Fourth Edition

A Writer's
WORKBOOK

A Writing Text with Readings

D1206134

TEACHER'S MANUAL

TRUDY SMOKE

CAMBRIDGE
UNIVERSITY PRESS

CAMBRIDGE UNIVERSITY PRESS
Cambridge, New York, Melbourne, Madrid, Cape Town,
Singapore, São Paulo, Delhi, Mexico City

Cambridge University Press
The Edinburgh Building, Cambridge CB2 8RU, UK

Published in the United States of America by Cambridge University Press, New York

www.cambridge.org
Information on this title: www.cambridge.org/9780521544900

© Cambridge University Press 2005

First published 2005

A catalogue record for this publication is available from the British Library

ISBN-13 978-0-521-54489-4 student's book
ISBN-10 0-521-54489-0 student's book
ISBN-13 978-0-521-54490-0 teacher's book
ISBN-10 0-521-54490-4 teacher's book

ISBN 978-0-521-54490-0 Paperback

CONTENTS

INTRODUCTION

A *Writer's Workbook* emphasizes development of the use of English for academic purposes. It integrates reading and writing activities, and it contains readings that typify the style of writing and vocabulary found in linguistics, sociology, psychology, and anthropology texts. The pedagogy in the book utilizes a collaborative and student-based approach, with many opportunities for students to work with a partner, in small groups, or with the entire class.

STRUCTURE OF THE STUDENT'S BOOK

A *Writer's Workbook* is divided into twelve chapters, which are grouped in four units: "Language," "Culture," "Work," and "Roots." Each chapter is divided into the following six sections:

Prereading
• an illustration related to the reading
• discussion questions to activate prior knowledge
• a vocabulary activity

Reading
• a brief biography of the writer
• the reading selection

Postreading
• questions to check comprehension and encourage discussion of ideas
• questions to provoke analysis of how the piece was written
• questions to elicit personal response

Writing
• journal writing
• presentation of one or more aspects of formal writing and related activities
• the main writing assignment
• a technique for getting started
• writing the first draft

Revising
• analysis and suggestions for revision of a sample piece of writing
• analysis and suggestions for revision of a partner's writing
• writing the second draft

Editing
• presentation of a grammar point and related activities
• editing the main writing assignment for grammar
• presentation of a mechanics point and related activities
• editing the main writing assignment for mechanics

TEACHING GUIDELINES

Prereading

Many teachers like to have students discuss what the illustration on the first page of the reading suggests because it is an enjoyable way to lead students into the topic of the reading. The discussion should focus on the illustration in a broad sense – on what it evokes and implies, rather than on merely describing its content.

Follow up students' ideas about the illustration with the discussion questions, which are designed to activate their prior knowledge about a topic and give them the opportunity to learn from others in the classroom. The questions are intended for the entire class, but some teachers prefer to ask students to work in small groups, where they discuss one or all of the questions and then share their answers with the class. Other teachers find it more effective to engage the entire class in discussing the questions, putting interesting information and new vocabulary on the board, and sometimes introducing visual materials (such as the map of a country or a relevant photo or chart) to build students' understanding and interest.

Vocabulary: Words in Context tasks appear in Chapters 1–11. Working with a partner, students figure out from context the meaning of the italicized words in three to five sentences or short passages excerpted from the text of the reading. Learning to derive the meaning of words from context is an important skill for students to build because they do not have time to look up every new word they encounter. Furthermore, looking up each new word would slow down the reading process and make it a frustrating experience.

Students gain vocabulary and reading skills, however, by a combination of strategies including figuring out word meanings from context, discussing words with their classmates, and using the dictionary. Many teachers, therefore, encourage students to verify their guesses at meaning by checking in the dictionary. Whichever way you choose to have students complete this activity, it is very important that they always perform the second part, in which they take turns explaining to a partner in their own words the meaning of the entire sentence or passage. It's a good idea to then call on a few students to repeat their explanations for the class.

You may want to suggest (or require) that students add new words to a "personal dictionary" that they keep either in their class notebook or a separate notebook. Have them add to this personal dictionary any new words they encounter in the readings or in class discussions. Encourage students to try to use some of these new words in their writing.

The reading in Chapter 12 is a short story containing specialized vocabulary relating to the southwestern United States and the Roman Catholic religion. Because it is unlikely that students will be able to guess the meanings of these words from context, the vocabulary activity for this chapter is different.

See page 61 of this manual for a discussion of the vocabulary task in Chapter 12.

Reading

In each unit, there are three reading selections, one per chapter. The first selection is a personal essay, the selection in the second chapter is an academic essay, and the third chapter uses either a journalistic selection or a piece of fiction. These choices were made to introduce students to the different styles in which people write according to their purposes and audiences.

Because students will have discussed some of the ideas in the reading selection and reviewed some of the vocabulary in class, teachers usually ask them to read the selection for the first time as homework. Of course, the first reading may also be done in class if you prefer. Some teachers read the selection aloud after students have read it on their own so that students can hear the correct pronunciation and intonation. If you choose to do this, students can even tape your readings so that they can listen to them at home.

In general, students benefit from reading the same selection several times. The first reading usually serves the purpose of getting a general idea of the piece; the next reading may be to look at specific features such as the introduction, cohesion between paragraphs, vocabulary, etc.; and a third reading would focus on the content and point of view of the author. Developing the habit of reading an academic text more than once is important, especially now that many colleges are requiring written exams based on comprehension of selected pieces of writing.

Postreading

Think about the Content questions, which follow each reading, are designed for small group discussions. Such discussions give students the opportunity to talk with each other about a common reading, to see how well they understood the reading, and to expand their understanding of it by hearing other responses. After the small group discussions, teachers often continue the discussion with the full class.

Think about the Writing questions are meant to be discussed as a class because it is important that all students hear each point made about writing. These questions lead students to analyze the writing itself and, it is hoped, apply some of the writing strategies to their own writing.

A *Personal Response* questions are intended for partner work and help students to think about their own experiences in relation to what they have read.

The suggestions mentioned above are only one way to use the postreading questions. Some teachers prefer discussing all the questions with the entire class; some ask different groups of students to work on different questions and then report their discussions to the class; other teachers assign all or some of the questions for homework to be discussed along with the selection in class. You might also consider assigning some of the questions for online class Web board discussions.

Writing

Journal Writing is helpful to students because it allows them to write freely without worrying about grammar, mechanics, spelling, or organization. To that end, students write a journal entry in response to each selection they read and discuss. This encourages them to develop the habit of writing about what they have read and of seeing writing as a tool for learning and exploring their ideas. The journal questions are meant to encourage students to think and then write about an aspect of the reading selection that touches them or corresponds to their own experience.

There are various ways to have students keep journals. One way is to have them write at home in a private journal that is collected periodically throughout the semester. If you choose this approach, you may permit your students to fold over any pages that are personal and that they do not want to share with you; this helps them understand that journals are personal learning tools. If you prefer, the journals may be written on the computer and e-mailed to you. In this case, students can omit from what they send you any parts of their journals they feel are too personal for anyone else to see. If you conduct part of your class using online activities, you may occasionally, with your students' permission, publish a student's journal entry in a chat room or blog so that other students can respond and have an online discussion. Another approach is to have students engage in a dialogue-style journal in which the student writes his or her response directly to you (as though the student were writing you a letter), and you in turn write back to each student. Whichever approach you choose, bear in mind that most researchers suggest you only comment on the content and not on the language, grammar, or mechanics when responding to students' journals.

From time to time, you may encounter students who do not want to keep a journal. You may decide to accept this, or you may give them a different assignment such as asking them to copy a part of the reading they especially liked and a part they especially disliked and write a brief explanation for their choices. This is not as personal as a typical journal entry, but it does get students into the habit of writing in response to reading.

With the exception of Chapter 1, which deals with autobiographical writing (see next paragraph), at least one type of *Formal Writing* that students are expected to produce during their academic careers is introduced in each chapter. The writing assignment for the chapter then has students practice that type of writing. For example, when students are introduced to how to write summaries, the writing assignment they do for that chapter is to write a summary; when students are introduced to the cause-and-effect essay, the writing assignment is a cause-and-effect essay, and so on. In some chapters, a second aspect of formal writing is also introduced – for example, paraphrasing or connecting ideas. Tasks that allow students to practice these skills are provided.

Students are offered three choices of topic for each writing assignment with the exception of Chapters 1 and 8. The writing assignment for Chapter 1 asks students to write an autobiographical essay that is structured around their experiences with reading and writing. For more information about the Chapter 1 assignment, see page 3 of this manual. In Chapter 8, students write a persuasive essay under test conditions and are offered two choices in accordance with the style of the test. For more information about the Chapter 8 assignment, see page 39 of this manual.

In each chapter, *Getting Started* introduces a technique that helps students with their writing assignments. Though a different technique is focused on in each chapter, not all work equally well for all students. In some chapters, you may want to allow students to use a technique they prefer rather than try the one presented, but have them try at least a few of the different techniques. This way they discover that there are many ways to get started even if a writing assignment seems difficult at first. In Chapters 5, 8, and 11, however, all students should do the *Getting Started* activities specific to those chapters because they are integral to the development of their essays.

Revising

After writing the first draft of their essays, students revise and then write a second draft. It is important for students to understand that revising necessarily consists of two steps: (1) analyzing both what is good and what needs improvement in a piece of writing, followed by (2) rewriting, i.e., adding to, deleting from, and reorganizing the piece of writing.

To provide practice in analyzing writing, students are given a task in which they are asked to analyze a sample essay and make suggestions for how it could be improved. This is such an important skill for students to learn that it is recommended that teachers model the task, perhaps working with a tutor or with one student. Students are often not sure how to work with a partner to make both positive and instructive comments, which is why modeling this process is enormously beneficial to them. It is interesting to note that although students often need time – and help from teachers – to become proficient at analyzing writing, many of my students have said they learned more about revising by doing this analysis than from any other activity.

The Student's Book provides a *Peer Response Form* (page 228) for students to reproduce and use each time they analyze writing – the writing of others as well as their own. Be sure to include the use of this form as you model how to analyze the writing of others. It is essential that you make students aware of how important it is to find and state the good points in a piece of writing before discussing the areas of weakness. (The order of questions in the *Peer Response Form* leads them to do this.) The purpose of revision is to improve a piece of writing, and writers who are encouraged by positive responses to their good points are usually more motivated to work on the weak ones. Let students know that if they need more room for their comments, they can either continue on the back of the form or use additional paper.

After students practice analyzing the writing of someone else, they work in pairs to analyze their own writing and then plan how to revise it. Each partner should fill out the *Peer Response Form* in relation to his or her partner's writing. Then they can use the two forms as the basis for their discussion. While students work with their partners, it is a good idea for you to walk from pair to pair, observing, listening, and offering guidance as needed.

Take some time to discuss with students how they should write their second drafts. It is critical for them to understand that in the end each writer must make his or her own decision as to how much of a partner's advice to take. Ideally, the analysis skills students are developing will help them distinguish good advice from bad. Partner feedback is important, but the final decisions about what and how to revise must be those of the individual writer. It often happens that students see ways to improve their own writing that their partners didn't see.

This is a good time to point out to students that in the "real" world, writers often revise many times for the simple reason that once doesn't always do the job. If time permits, you should feel free to allow students to write more than two drafts. One possibility is to have students revise once, give them written feedback, and even grade their papers. Then allow them to revise once more, bearing your comments in mind. This approach gives students excellent practice as well as a chance for a better grade. (See more about assessing your students' writing under *Suggestions for Responding to Students' Writing* on page xii.)

Editing

Up to this point in *A Writer's Workbook*, students have concentrated on the content and organization of their writing. In the *Editing* section, students work on elements of writing that are often intimidating to them: grammar and mechanics.

The *Grammar* section of each chapter presents an aspect of grammar that typically poses problems for students when they write. Practice exercises in which students apply the grammar follow its presentation. The last practice exercise is always a paragraph with errors in the grammar discussed in the chapter; students must correct these errors and then check their answers in the back of the Student's Book. Answers for the other grammar tasks are in this manual.

At the end of the *Grammar* section, students are given instructions to edit their own writing for grammar. This is done in two steps: First, students review their writing looking for errors in the grammatical aspect presented in the chapter. Then they are told to choose two or three other areas of grammar that typically give them problems and look for errors in these areas. You may want to ask students to note at the bottom of their papers which grammar areas they chose to look for in addition to the one addressed in the chapter. As you become familiar with your students' writing, you can help them identify their problem areas.

The *Mechanics* section of each chapter includes information about such topics as how to use commas and semicolons, how to avoid run-on sentences and fragments, and how to punctuate direct speech. As in the *Grammar* section, a mechanics point is presented and followed by practice exercises, the last of which is a paragraph that needs editing for the specific mechanics issue discussed in the chapter. (Answers for the paragraph to be edited appear in the back of the Student's Book.)

Each chapter ends with a checklist, *Edit Your Writing for Mechanics*, a tool that requires students to review their writing for each mechanics point discussed from Chapter 1 through the chapter on which they are working. You may want students to copy this checklist onto a piece of paper and hand it in with their essays.

Naturally, there is a somewhat arbitrary order for the grammar and mechanics issues discussed in each chapter. You may want to use them in a different order or you may decide to assign particular ones to individual students or small groups of students.

SUGGESTIONS FOR CREATING A COMMUNICATIVE CLASSROOM ENVIRONMENT

- As students work together in the classroom, circulate among them observing, listening, and giving guidance when necessary. Talk to the groups and show interest in the conversation.

- Provide opportunities for quieter students to interact by having students work with partners, in small groups, or by using a class Web board and chat room. Having an online connection for the class may encourage students who are reluctant to speak in class to communicate on the computer either to you personally or to their classmates. Write to the students online in response to their entries and also to pose and answer questions. You may want to schedule a particular day and time when you will be available on the computer for a class chat.

- In every class meeting, try to ensure that each student has an opportunity to speak to the whole class or to a small group, even if only for 2 or 3 minutes. In addition to the activities in the book, you can ask students to find newspaper articles related to the chapter topic and present the information in the article to the class; or, you may divide students into teams to debate an issue related to the topic.

SUGGESTIONS FOR RESPONDING TO STUDENTS' WRITING

- Use students' journals as a form of dialogue. Respond with interest to what they have written rather than simply writing "good" or "interesting," and so on.

- Read each student's essay through once before responding or correcting. Respond to the content and organization first with extended written comments that point out the strengths of the writing as well as the weaknesses. Many teachers do this by writing a short paragraph at the end of the essay that is a note to the student rather than by inserting comments throughout the paper. Then respond to the grammar and mechanics. Let students know what they do well and then where their weak points are.

- Put a dot at the edge of each line where there is an error in grammar or mechanics and ask students to work with a partner to find the problem. (If they cannot find the problem, they need to ask you.)

- Consider the option of responding to students' drafts via audiotape. Rather than writing on a draft, you can record your ongoing response to the content and organization as you read.

- Grade papers so that students understand their strengths and weaknesses. One way of doing this is to give a triple grade – one grade for content and organization, one for grammar, and one for mechanics. Some teachers average these into one grade. They then encourage students to write additional drafts addressing the area where they have the most problems, which gives them a chance to raise their grade.

- Require your students to meet one-on-one with you to go over one of their essays at least once per semester (preferably more than once). Some teachers do this at midterm time and then again a few weeks before the end of the semester. Have students read parts of their essay aloud to you; many times students self correct when they read.

- Have students keep copies of their multiple drafts so that you and they can compare the changes and improvements in their writing.

- Have students keep portfolios of their writing throughout the semester so you and they can track their growth.

PLANNING YOUR COURSE

A *Writer's Workbook* works well with a variety of writing classes. It may be used in six-week, twelve-week, or fourteen-week semesters. It may be used in intensive language classes as well as classes that meet less frequently.

Although there is a progression in the formal writing presented and practiced in each chapter, teachers are not bound to follow the order of the book. The units do not have to be taught in the order in which they occur, nor do all three chapters of a unit have to be taught.

Some teachers may choose to have students complete only the chapters with academic readings (Chapters 2, 5, 8, and 11) while still doing all the *Grammar* and *Mechanics* sections in the book. Other teachers may decide to have students complete the *Grammar* and *Mechanics* sections selectively or even assign them individually or to small groups of students. Still other teachers may want to focus on the personal essay at the beginning of the semester, in which case they would have students do Chapters 1, 4, 7, and 10 first. Teachers who prefer to have students read one genre at a time may organize their semester by first assigning chapters with personal essays, then focusing on chapters with journalistic essays (Chapters 3 and 9), followed by academic essays, and concluding with fiction (Chapters 6 and 12).

Depending on the length of your semester and how many hours a week your class meets, you might spend one or two weeks on a chapter. Some teachers focus on *Prereading*, *Reading*, and *Postreading* for the first two classes and then focus on *Writing* in the next class. The *Revising*, *Grammar*, and *Mechanics* sections are then done in the following class. In that way, a chapter may be used for two weeks.

There is a great deal of flexibility in how you choose to use *A Writer's Workbook*. The *Plan of the Book*, on pages vi–xiii of the Student's Book, and the *Index*, on pages 248–249 of the Student's Book, permit you to easily see all the readings and activities with the page(s) where they may be found. These features will help you personalize the book to meet class needs and plan a syllabus that works effectively for an eight-week, twelve-week, fourteen-week, or longer program. What makes this book work so well for so many different kinds of teachers and students is the breadth of material presented and the variety of activities and readings.

UNIT ONE
Language

Chapter One
Chapter One

DESTINATION: COLLEGE, U.S.A.

"Destination: College, U.S.A.," by Yilu Zhao, is a personal essay about the culture shock felt by a student who left her home in China to come to the United States to study at Yale University.

PREREADING (pages 2–3)

See page vi of this manual for teaching guidelines about prereading and reading.

Begin by asking students to look at the illustration on page 2. Encourage them to discuss what it suggests about being a college student. How is the work in college different from that in high school? What methods do college students use to study, read textbooks, and organize their time? Students who are entering college for the first time can contrast their high school experiences with their expectations for college. Students who have gone to schools in other countries can contrast their experiences in those places with what they have found or expect to find in U.S. colleges. Then discuss the questions on page 2 with the class.

The vocabulary task on page 3 presents passages taken from the text. Students should attempt to figure out the meaning of the italicized sections from the context. If they cannot, they should feel free to use the dictionary. It is important, however, that students practice explaining the meaning of each passage in their own words.

POSTREADING (page 7)

See page vii of this manual for teaching guidelines about postreading.

Think about the Content (page 7)

1 Yilu Zhao grew up in China; the typical Yalie grew up in the United States. Yilu Zhao does not come from a privileged background as do many of the students at Yale. Her cultural background and references are different from the students there as well. She does not understand the jokes or the slang,

1

nor does she know about grills and American eating customs. Her study habits are also different from those of many of the students at Yale. She is a serious student who puts in long hours at the library and is less interested than her classmates in social life.

2 Yilu Zhao finds the classroom atmosphere to be very different from what she knew in China.

> The professors [at Yale] do not teach in the same way that teachers in China do. Studying humanities in China means memorizing all the "correct," standard interpretations given during lectures. [Yale] professors toss out provocative questions and let the students argue, research and write papers on their own. At Yale, I often waited for the end-of-class "correct" answers, which never came. (Par. 13)

> Learning humanities was well-grounded repetition in China, but it was shaky originality here. And it could be even shakier for me. (Par. 14)

3 Zhao studies very hard, often staying late in the college library. ". . . I visited the writing tutor . . . for every paper I turned in. My papers were always written days before they were due." She stays after class to ask questions of her professors and she borrows classmates' notes to "learn the skill of note-taking in English." (Par. 17)

Think about the Writing (page 7)

1 Zhao begins with a detailed story that puts the reader in her position. She concludes her story with a provocative last line: "And that is when I started to panic." The reader wants to know what she does to handle her panic.

2 She describes the way students around her talked and explains that she could not understand some of their slangy expressions such as "Like I . . ." She does not know what a grill is. She does not understand the jokes that other students are laughing about.

3 Paragraphs 4–8 include many details of Zhao's life in China. Here are some of them: She tells us that her father is a government clerk and her mother works in a textile factory. She describes her mother's difficult working conditions and explains that she spent a whole year's salary to pay for Zhao's flight to the United States. Zhao lived in a high school dormitory with eight students to a room. Her grandparents' one-room apartment was bigger than the apartment she shared with her parents. She studied and memorized to prepare for qualifying exams. When she was a child, her mother told her she could "do anything and be anyone." Her family expects a lot from her.

At Yale, she is on her own. She is lonely and unfamiliar with the food. She is homesick for her family. She spends most of her time studying instead of socializing. She tries some American foods but does not like them as much as the food she grew up eating. She enrolls in courses that she knows will be hard for her but that will introduce her to Western culture and its canons of philosophy, literature, and history.

A Personal Response (page 7)

Answers may vary.

WRITING (pages 7–9)

See page viii of this manual for teaching guidelines about writing.

Journal Writing (page 7)

Remind students to use their journals as a place to reflect and think without worrying about spelling, grammar, or the mechanics of writing.

Formal Writing: *Autobiographical Essay* (page 8)

In this chapter, students write an autobiographical essay focused on their experiences as readers and writers. This type of essay is useful for teachers as well as students. It helps students identify their strengths and the areas in which they need to do more work. Teachers benefit from a personal introduction to each student and an overview of the strengths and needs of their class. Most of the other writing students do as they work in this book will be less personal, but the autobiographical essay is an effective way to begin the course.

Getting Started: *Freewriting* (page 9)

Most students find freewriting to be a useful technique that they use throughout their college experience. Freewriting is especially helpful for students who feel blocked or who have trouble beginning their writing. As an introduction to this activity, it will be helpful for students if you model the technique on the board. Some teachers also like to freewrite along with their students.

REVISING (pages 9–11)

See page ix of this manual for teaching guidelines about revising.

The questions on page 11 are meant to help direct your students into thinking about revising in a constructive way and also to help them become aware of essay organization.

Before students begin to analyze the essay on pages 10–11, you might want to model how to do this, working together with a student or class tutor.

After you have discussed the first paragraph of the essay (question 1), it is important to remind students to point out something good about the essay before they begin to make suggestions for changes.

Finding something good in the essay is the explicit point of question 2. You might amplify question 2 by asking students to decide what word, sentence, or idea they like best.

The purpose of question 3 is to elicit from students whether there are any parts of the essay that are not successful – parts that could be eliminated, expanded, or done in a different way. Students should be able to explain their choices.

In most chapters, students analyze their writing by filling out a *Peer Response Form*. In this chapter, therefore, it is advisable to have partners analyze each other's essays by responding to the four questions in writing. A written response gives the responder additional writing practice and also provides a document the essay writer can refer to as he or she revises.

EDITING (pages 12–17)

See page x of this manual for teaching guidelines about editing.

Grammar: *Appropriate Tenses for Expressing Past Time* (pages 12–15)

Understanding the various methods for expressing past experiences is critical to reading and writing. Because the writing for this chapter involves reflecting on events in the past, we begin with this review of how to express past time. Some teachers approach the past tenses by having students look at a piece of writing and underlining the past tense verbs; others begin by reviewing the rules. If you decide to look at writing, use Zhao's essay and the student essay on pages 10–11. In the student essay, begin with paragraph 2 since paragraph 1 relies heavily on the passive voice.

Many students like grammar charts because they provide a fast visual aid. You could create a chart such as the one below for regular verbs, adding as many verbs as you feel would be helpful. If you create this chart on the board, elicit as much help as possible from the class in building it. (Refer students to the chart on pages 231–234 of the Student's Book for the simple past tenses of irregular verbs.) You can add to this chart examples for each of the six tenses discussed in the chapter: simple past, past progressive, present perfect, present perfect progressive, past perfect, and past perfect progressive. Creating a chart may be too easy for many of your students. If so, assign it only as necessary – perhaps to a small group working with a tutor.

	Statement	Negative	Interrogative
Simple Past	I worked.	I did not work.	Did I work?
	etc.		
Past Progressive	I was working.	I was not working.	Was I working?
	etc.		

1 *had always lived* (past perfect); *had never traveled* (past perfect); *won* (simple past); *was* (simple past); *had wanted* (past perfect); *decided* (simple past); *studied* (simple past); *was living* (past progressive); *visited* (simple past)

2 *has studied* (present perfect); *studied* (simple past); *lived* (simple past); *heard* (simple past); *was studying* (past progressive); *invited* (simple past); *graduated* (simple past); *arrived* (simple past); *had been studying* (past perfect progressive)

3 *read* (simple past); *found* (simple past); *went* (simple past); *took* (simple past); *started* (simple past); *am working* (present progressive); *have gone* (present perfect); *spent* (simple past); *had been hoping* (past perfect progressive)

GRAMMAR PRACTICE 2 (pages 14–15)

Answers will vary. Here are some possible answers.

1 *has traveled*; *got*
2 *had done*; *received*; *was*
3 *has been*; *saw*
4 *was doing*; *knocked*; *wanted*
5 *did not read*; *took*
6 *ate*; *lived*; *has been*

GRAMMAR PRACTICE 3 (page 15)

See *Answer Key* in Student's Book, page 235.

Mechanics: *Paper Format* (pages 16–17)

In this chapter, students learn the standard format for papers. You may want to modify some of these instructions to fit your own requirements. Be sure that students make use of the editing checklist on page 17 before they hand in their autobiographical essays.

Chapter Two

HOW TO BE A SUCCESSFUL LANGUAGE LEARNER

"How to Be a Successful Language Learner" is an excerpt from a research study by Anita L. Wenden that describes a variety of learning strategies used by learners of English at Columbia University. The study makes the point that all people do not learn in exactly the same way.

PREREADING (pages 18–19)

See page vi of this manual for teaching guidelines about prereading and reading.

Begin by having students discuss what seems to be going on in the illustration on page 18. What are idioms? Why are they important to know? Then discuss the questions on page 18, which will help students realize how much they already know about methods of learning a language.

The vocabulary task on page 19 presents passages taken from the text. Students should attempt to figure out the meaning of the italicized words from the context. If they cannot, they should feel free to use the dictionary. It is important, however, that students practice explaining the meaning of each passage in their own words.

POSTREADING (pages 24–25)

See page vii of this manual for teaching guidelines about postreading.

Think about the Content (page 24)

1 Answers may vary.
2 Answers may vary.
3 If someone translates exactly word for word, the translation may not have the same meaning as the original.
4 Answers may vary.

Think about the Writing (page 24)

1 The italicized words describe the theme of the paragraph that will follow.

2 Reading original quotes gives the reader a sense of the actual students. If Wenden had summarized these, the personality and individuality of the particular students would have been lost. Retaining the flavor of the interviewee is one reason some writers prefer to quote from their sources rather than to paraphrase.

3 The students are described in paragraph 1. Answers may vary as to whether this is the best placement of this information. If students suggest a different place, elicit why their proposed placement would be better.

4 Wenden explains the significance of her study in paragraph 18, the last paragraph. She states: "The beliefs point to the fact that these learners have begun to reflect upon what they are doing in order to understand the principles behind it." Answers may vary as to whether this is the best placement of this information and as to whether this best sums up the significance of the study. As with the response to number 3, if students disagree with Wenden's placement of this information, have them explain their reasons.

A Personal Response (pages 24–25)

| Answers may vary.

WRITING (pages 25–29)

See page viii of this manual for teaching guidelines about writing.

Journal Writing (page 25)

Remind students to use their journals as a place to reflect and think without worrying about spelling, grammar, or the mechanics of writing.

Formal Writing: *Introduction to the Academic Essay* (pages 25–26)

On page 26 there is a graphic illustration of a typical five-paragraph academic essay. It is important to point out to students that all essays do not have to be five paragraphs, but that this graphic is meant simply to illustrate the basic components of the essay: introduction, development, and conclusion.

Formal Writing: *Compare and Contrast Essay* (pages 27–28)

Two methods for writing compare and contrast essays are introduced on pages 27–28: the block pattern and the alternating points pattern. As with the academic essay, a graphic illustration helps students understand the two methods – and their differences. Following each illustration, sample paragraphs in that method are provided. Students can work as a class or in small groups to read the examples and decide which pattern works better for their topic. You may also want to use the sample paragraphs as springboards for students to develop a longer essay on the topic of the sample paragraphs: whether living at home or away from home is better for college students. This could be done in class in small groups or as a homework assignment.

The writing assignment topics on page 29 call on students to compare and contrast two systems or strategies. Assignment choice 2 can be developed into a longer paper in which students do some research or work with a group of students speaking the same language to compare and contrast the characteristics of a particular language with English. Sometimes students become so interested in this topic that they want to make class presentations about it. Having students present on a topic about which they know something provides them with an excellent experience in showing their strengths and also in helping them to realize how much they know.

Getting Started: *Making Lists* (page 29)

In this chapter, the lists students make are meant to aid them in organizing their compare and contrast essays; however, lists can be used for other academic purposes as well. You may want to ask students in what other academic context they use lists (e.g., for what particular subjects are lists useful as a study aid? how might lists be of assistance in tasks that require memorization?) This discussion fits in well with the overall topic of different learning styles and approaches to academic success.

REVISING (pages 30–32)

See page ix of this manual for teaching guidelines about revising.

Students begin this section by reading two drafts of an essay, analyzing how it changed, and deciding which draft they prefer and why. Then they analyze and revise their own essays.

In this chapter, students use the *Peer Response Form* on pages 228–229 of the Student's Book for the first time. The form is photocopiable and each student should use a clean copy for each essay he or she reads. Review the form with students before they begin the activities. Point out the places where they are asked to describe the strength of a draft and those where they are asked to make suggestions for change. Show students that after the first question, which asks them to address the general organization of the essay, they are asked to focus on the strengths of the essay before they discuss the places that need work. Encourage students to use the peer response process to improve the content of their essays; they should not dwell on problems in grammar and mechanics unless these interfere with meaning.

The revising sections of this book are designed to help students develop the language and skills to analyze and to describe their (and others') writing and to make decisions about revising that go beyond just correcting a few errors and moving a few words. Advise students that if there isn't enough room on the form for all their comments, they can write on the back of the form or use additional paper.

EDITING (pages 32–38)

See page x of this manual for teaching guidelines about editing.

Grammar: *Using the Present Tenses* (pages 33–35)

Understanding the various uses of the present tenses is critical to becoming proficient in English. Skill in manipulating these tenses allows writers (and speakers) to express subtle differences in meaning.

GRAMMAR PRACTICE 1 (page 34)

1 *has been teaching* (present perfect progressive); *does not always interview* (simple present); *describes* (simple present); *has discovered* (present perfect); *have been studying* (present perfect progressive); *using* (present perfect progressive); *believe* (simple present); *is* (simple present); *read, study, listen* (simple present); *write* (simple present); *is trying* (present progressive); *is* (simple present); *is* (simple present); *think* (simple present); *are* (simple present); *is* (simple present); *has learned* (present perfect); *shares* (simple present)

2 *study* (simple present); *are approaching* (present progressive); *are* (simple present); *know* (simple present); *have* (simple present); *are* (simple present); *use* (simple present); *talk* (simple present); *are eating, playing, working* (present progressive); *studying* (present progressive); *talk* (simple present); *talk* (simple present); *talk* (simple present); *talk* (simple present); *becomes* (simple present); *are studying* (present progressive)

GRAMMAR PRACTICE 2 (pages 34–35)

Answers may vary. Here are some possible answers.

1 *teaches*; *has taught*; *is*
2 *read*; *helps*; *require*; *believe*; *knows*; *is*
3 *think*; *means*; *think*; *means*; *discover*; *means*

Grammar: *Subject-Verb Agreement in the Simple Present Tense* (pages 35–38)

The biggest problem with the simple present tense is usually the third person -*s* inflection. The first thing students need to do to alleviate this problem is to be able to identify the subject of the sentence and determine whether it is singular or plural. Many students think a plural subject should be followed by a "plural" verb, which they believe is a verb ending in an *s*. Of course, it is just the opposite in English. Sometimes it helps these students to tell them that in general if the subject of a sentence ends in *s* then the verb does not. This does not always work, however; some singular nouns end in *s* and some plural nouns do not, but it is a start. Students also enjoy discovering the exceptions.

GRAMMAR PRACTICE 3 (pages 36–37)

1 Students in a standard six-year Chinese high school *take* five years of physics, four years of chemistry, and three years of biology.

2 Listening and speaking are both necessary to develop good pronunciation. (Correct)

3 No one likes to be called on when he or she is not prepared. (Correct)

4 Learning English, whether in a college or in other types of schools or programs, is a challenge for many students. (Correct)

5 The government *works* to ensure the safety of its citizens.

6 Either my older brother or my parents *help* me with my homework. [Note: The subject of the sentence consists of nouns joined by the conjunctions *either . . . or*. The verb should agree with the noun that is closer to it, *parents*.]

7 Laptop computers, which are used by students in many parts of the world, allow people to take notes, read pages, and even go on the Internet. (Correct)

[Note: The verbs *to take, read,* and *go* are understood to be in the infinitive form and do not require inflectional endings. You may want to point out that even though *read* and *go* are not preceded by the word *to,* they are understood to be infinitives because they directly follow the infinitive *to take.*]

8 Linguists <u>agree</u> that there <u>are</u> no superior or inferior languages.
[Note: The phrase *"no superior or inferior languages"* is the extraposed subject, that is a subject that is moved out of the subject position from the normal subject-verb-object (SVO) English type of sentence. *There* functions as a placeholder for the subject, and students need to look at what follows the verb to find the subject and then make sure the verb agrees with the subject. Here are some sentences for students to use as practice with *there*:
There _____ two cars ahead of me on line for the toll.
There _____ an opening for a roommate in my apartment.
There _____ a free ticket waiting for you at the box office.
There _____ a few empty seats in the auditorium.]

9 Either the door or the windows <u>need</u> to be opened to cool off the room. (Correct)
[Note: See number 6 above.]

10 <u>Reading, writing, speaking, and listening</u> to a new language <u>are</u> necessary to learn it. (Correct)

11 <u>The library and the Internet</u> *help* students find information.

12 <u>Nobody</u> *wants* to fail a course.

13 <u>I</u> <u>notice</u> that there <u>are</u> always <u>lots of people</u> waiting for the bus at five o'clock. (Correct)
[Note: See number 8 above.]

14 When <u>I</u> <u>write</u> an essay, either <u>my teacher or the tutors</u> in my English class <u>go</u> over it with me.

15 <u>My neighbors</u>, who usually drive me to work in the morning, <u>are</u> out of town, so <u>I</u> <u>have</u> to take the bus. (Correct)

16 <u>The band and the singer</u> *are* great!

17 <u>The drama club</u> <u>goes</u> to two plays every month. (Correct)

18 <u>The children's choir</u> <u>sings</u> with the adult choir on holidays. (Correct)

19 There <u>are</u> <u>a painting and a drawing</u> by Picasso in our local museum.

20 <u>My aunt and uncle, my cousins, and my grandmother</u> *come* to our house for dinner every Sunday.

GRAMMAR PRACTICE **4** (pages 37–38)

See *Answer Key* in Student's Book, page 235.

Mechanics: *Using Quotation Marks, Brackets, and Ellipses* (pages 38–41)

In this chapter, students focus on the use of quotation marks, brackets, and ellipses, which are used in abundance in the Wenden text. Students are asked to notice how Wenden uses these marks of punctuation, but you may also want students to look at a newspaper or magazine article or a short story to see how other writers have used these forms. It is often useful, especially for students having difficulty with a grammar or mechanics form, to look at another piece of writing, underline the use of the particular form, and then analyze why the form was used. If the students find errors, this can lead to a useful discussion as well. You can also have students analyze previous writing of their own and decide if they have used a particular form correctly.

MECHANICS PRACTICE 1 (page 40)

1 The quotation marks indicate the name of the article. Quotation marks are used with the names of articles, book chapters, essays, poems, short stories, and songs. Titles of books, movies, operas, plays, magazines, and newspapers are set off in italics or with underlines if they are handwritten.

2 Question marks belong inside the quotation marks. Single quotation marks are used to indicate a quote within a quote.

3 Sometimes it is necessary to add or alter words in a quotation for clarification or to make the context clearer. The author uses brackets to indicate that she is adding words to clarify what relationship Miguel is talking about. You must always bracket any words in a quotation that you add or alter.

4 The four periods after *accounting* indicate that words have been deleted from a quotation after the end of that sentence. If words are deleted beginning in the middle of a sentence, only an ellipsis (three periods) is added. For example, if the deletion had started after the word *business,* there would only be an ellipsis.

5 Words have been deleted after a comma appeared in the original quotation.

MECHANICS PRACTICE 2 (page 41)

See *Answer Key* in Student's Book, page 236.

Chapter Three

THE EDUCATION OF BERENICE BELIZAIRE

In his magazine article, "The Education of Berenice Belizaire," Joe Klein tells the story of a young girl who immigrates from Haiti to the United States with her mother and sister and succeeds despite many obstacles – both financial and social.

PREREADING (pages 42–43)

See page vi of this manual for teaching guidelines about prereading and reading.

Students who particularly enjoy reading about Berenice Belizaire may want to read books by Edwidge Danticat in which she tells the (often sad) stories of Haitian immigrants. If they are interested in stories of immigrants, they may enjoy reading the memoirs of Esmeralda Santiago, Maxine Hong Kingston, or Mark Mathabane; or the fiction of Cristina Garcia, Chang-Rae Lee, Gus Lee, Oscar Hijuelos, or Julia Alvarez among many others.

As a change of pace, begin by having your students write for 5 minutes about the illustration on page 42. What is happening in the picture? Ask them to write the story of one of the people. What is going on? What does the event seem to mean to the person they are writing about? Or ask them to write about what they remember about their high school graduation. What was the significance of that day to them? Have them share their writing with a small group. Then let each group either select one piece of writing to read to the class or exchange their writing with another group.

Continue the lesson with a discussion of the questions on page 42. Here is some information that may be useful for the first question.

> Haiti is an independent republic in the Caribbean Sea; it occupies the western third of the island Hispaniola (the east portion is the Dominican Republic). People in Haiti speak Creole and French. Haiti has undergone much political tumult during its history. In 1492, Columbus arrived and claimed Hispaniola for Spain. Within the next twenty-five years, the Arawak, native to the area when Columbus arrived, were virtually annihilated.

> France took an interest in the area, and in 1697 the western third of the island was ceded to France. It became a plantation to which African slaves were imported. In 1791, a slave revolt of some half million slaves was led by Toussaint l'Ouverture. In 1804, Haiti became the first black republic to declare its independence. Jacques Dessalines was Haiti's first president.

After some political chaos, the United States occupied Haiti from 1915–1934. In 1957, François Duvalier became dictator and held power until his death in 1971. His son Jean-Claude, "Baby Doc," succeeded him but was ousted in 1986. Jean-Bertrand Aristide was elected president in 1990; he was ousted by a military regime, and then re-elected. Under pressure, Aristide resigned on February 29, 2004. As of July 2005, the interim president is Boniface Alexandre and the interim Prime Minister is Gérard Latortue.

The vocabulary task on page 43 presents passages taken from the text. Students should attempt to figure out the meaning of the italicized sections from the context. If they cannot, they should feel free to use the dictionary. It is important, however, that students practice explaining the meaning of each passage in their own words.

POSTREADING (page 46)

See page vii of this manual for teaching guidelines about postreading.

Think about the Content (page 46)

1 Berenice Belizaire and her family had a hard time when they first moved to Brooklyn, New York. They spoke no English, lived in a cramped apartment, and the mother worked long hours. Berenice endured taunts from students in her school, including being cursed at and having food thrown at her in the school cafeteria. Her sister was even hit in the head with a book. Yet the family could not return to Haiti where life would have been even more dangerous and educational opportunities would have been limited. (Par. 1)

2 Within two years, Berenice was speaking English. She was very successful in high school, especially in math. By her senior year, she was first in her class and was chosen as valedictorian. She was admitted to Massachusetts Institute of Technology and dreamed of becoming famous in the field of computer science. Answers may vary as to what explains these changes. Joe Klein explains some of the reasons for them: Berenice took extra summer classes to help her understand more; she got to know some of her teachers even though she was quiet; ". . . she always seemed to ask the right questions. She understood the big ideas. She could think on her feet. She could explain difficult problems . . . she was hungry for *knowledge*." (Par. 3)

3 According to Klein, immigrant energy has invigorated schools and teachers and possibly "reinvigorated the city itself in the 1980s." Immigrants restored the retail life of the city by starting small businesses. They worked hard at entry level jobs such as nursing assistants. They added more to the economy than they took from it. (Par. 6)

4 Answers may vary.

Think about the Writing (page 46)

1 Answers may vary.

2 Answers may vary.

3 Klein makes the transition in paragraph 6 although he quotes from one of Berenice's teachers in paragraph 5 to make a general comment about the value of immigrant energy and hard work. In paragraph 6, Klein quotes from a New York University professor. He quotes from an immigration counselor in paragraph 7, and he quotes from a man affiliated with Williams College in paragraph 8. These quotes support his main idea that immigrants are invigorating and reenergizing America rather than taking from it as may be popularly thought. Adding quotations from knowledgeable people adds to the credibility of a writer's opinions and ideas.

A Personal Response (page 46)

Answers may vary.

WRITING (pages 47–50)

See page viii of this manual for teaching guidelines about writing.

Journal Writing (page 47)

Remind students to use their journals as a place to reflect and think without worrying about spelling, grammar, or the mechanics of writing.

Formal Writing: *Introductions* (pages 47–49)

Student writers often fall into the habit of starting every paper in a similar way – finding a boilerplate introduction and sticking with it. To help students change this habit, this chapter presents examples of different types of introductions. *Formal Writing* Practice 2 asks students to practice changing the style of an introduction they have written. Encourage them to continue experimenting by changing that introduction to yet another style or by changing the style of other introductions they have written. They can discuss with a partner or a small group the effect of each. In later assignments, you can add to the revision task instructions that ask students to change the style of their introduction and then decide whether they prefer the new one or the original one. This will help students build flexibility and gain confidence in their writing.

Point out to students that all three of the main purposes an introduction serves that are listed on page 47 are not necessarily present in every introduction.

Formal Writing: *Process Essay* (pages 49–50)

The process essay is often included in composition texts because it helps students learn to break down complex tasks or experiences into steps. This helps not only in writing but also as a strategy for learning. You can introduce students to this mode of thinking by having them explain any complex daily task following the process described in the bulleted list at the bottom of page 49. It is sometimes fun, for example, to ask students to write down step-by-step how they get from school to their home, how they get from each class to the next, or how they make a new friend. Students usually enjoy suggesting ideas for activities they want to break down into steps. They can work as a class, in small groups, or as partners.

Getting Started: *Talking with a Partner* (page 50)

Students often say they learn more from talking with their partners or in small groups than in any other way. In these situations, language becomes more relaxed and comfortable. Students do not have to worry about being understood in the same way as they do when raising their hands in class. So this *Getting Started* activity may become one that students find especially valuable and one they may want to do again.

REVISING (pages 50–53)

See page ix of this manual for teaching guidelines about revising.

The essay on pages 51–53 was chosen because of its clear organization and because it offers good tips for students who are new to college. Students may find some redundancies and may be able to tighten the essay to make it even stronger, but overall, they should find the essay's message useful.

EDITING (pages 53–58)

See page x of this manual for teaching guidelines about editing.

Grammar: *Pronoun-Antecedent Agreement* (pages 53–56)

Even though students may be familiar with the rules for simple pronoun-antecedent agreement, many have problems with some of the more complex uses of pronouns. This section describes and gives students practice with some of the complications of pronoun agreement: agreement with a compound antecedent, two antecedents connected by *either/or* or *neither/nor*, an antecedent preceded by words such as *each* and *every*, an antecedent as an indefinite pronoun, an antecedent as a collective noun, and an antecedent followed by a relative clause. This section also addresses the issue of sexism and pronoun-antecedent agreement as well as three special pronoun problems.

GRAMMAR PRACTICE 1 (page 55)

1 *her*	4 *her*
2 *it*; *their*	5 *him*; *her*
3 *its*	

1 Antecedent: *Every student*   Pronoun: *His*
   This could be considered sexist unless the class is all male. Here is a possible revision: *All students* in my class are required to hand in an early draft of *their* term papers.

2 Antecedent: *My teacher*   Pronoun: *Her*

3 Antecedent: *Anyone*   Pronouns: *his, him*
   This could be considered sexist unless the class is all male. Here is a possible revision: *All students* can offer *their* opinions in my class, but we will not necessarily agree with *every opinion*.

4 Antecedent 1: *Each individual*   Pronoun: *her*
   This could be considered sexist unless all people involved are women. Here are possible revisions: *Each individual* who faces challenges has *his or her* own way of dealing with them. OR All people who face challenges have their own ways of dealing with them.
   Antecedent 2: *challenges*   Pronoun: *them*

5 Antecedent 1: *each twin*   Pronoun: *them* (refers to both of the twins)

   Antecedent 2: *each one*   Pronoun: *his* (This is not sexist because both twins are the same sex and probably male. If the twins were both female, the pronoun would be *her*.)

Grammar: *Three Special Pronoun Problems* (pages 56–58)

The issues addressed in this section do not fit neatly into any standard presentation of the pronoun system in English. However, they deal with common misunderstandings that students have about pronouns.

See *Answer Key* in Student's Book, page 236.

Mechanics: *Capitalization* (pages 58–59)

Although it is important for students to learn the rules for capitalization in English, it is also important for them to realize that all languages do not use capitals in the same way. You can use this lesson as an opportunity to have them discuss some of the differences in capitalization rules in other languages your students may speak.

See *Answer Key* in Student's Book, page 237.

UNIT TWO
Culture

Chapter Four
CULTURAL IDENTITY VS. ETHNIC FASHIONS

"Cultural Identity vs. Ethnic Fashions" is a personal essay by Sunita Puri, who identifies herself as being "a patchwork of different cultures." Through the lens of her own multiple identities, she criticizes the use of traditional cultural and religious symbols as fashion items in contemporary society.

PREREADING (pages 62–63)

See page vi of this manual for teaching guidelines about prereading and reading.

Begin by asking your students to look at the illustration on page 62. If no one in your class is aware of the cultural significance of the dot that appears on the forehead of the woman in the picture, tell them that it is a *bindi*, worn by Hindu women as a religious symbol that signifies female energy, or *Shakti*. The word *bindi* comes from *bindu*, the Sanskrit word for "drop." Some additional questions to discuss with your students: What else do they notice in the drawing? What may be the significance of placing the woman in an urban setting? What aspects of life are juxtaposed in the drawing? What does this drawing suggest the reading will be about? What do you know about the roles of women in different parts of the world? In what ways have the roles of women changed during the last century? Then discuss the questions on page 62 with the class.

The vocabulary task on page 63 presents passages taken from the text. Students should attempt to figure out the meaning of the italicized sections from the context. If they cannot, they should feel free to use the dictionary. It is important, however, that students practice explaining the meaning of each passage in their own words.

POSTREADING (pages 65–66)

See page vii of this manual for guidelines about postreading.

Think about the Content (page 65)

| Answers may vary.

Think about the Writing (pages 65–66)

| 1 Although answers may vary, most readers would agree that the main point is expressed in paragraph 7: "Assigning new cultural meanings to symbols with very old traditions or deep personal significance is inappropriate and insensitive."
| 2 Answers may vary.
| 3 Answers may vary.

A Personal Response (page 66)

| Answers may vary.

WRITING (pages 66–68)

See page viii of this manual for teaching guidelines about writing.

Journal Writing (page 66)

Remind students to use their journals as a place to reflect and think without worrying about spelling, grammar, or the mechanics of writing.

Formal Writing: *Conclusions* (page 66)

In this chapter, students learn about writing conclusions. This is a part of the essay that students sometimes neglect. Many fall into using clichéd phrases like "In conclusion" followed by a restatement of the main idea. This is one technique, but it is important for students to realize that it is only one. Encourage your class to study and discuss the conclusions of essays in this book, essays they and their classmates have written, and essays in other books, magazines, and newspapers. The more that students realize that writing offers creative options, the more comfortable they will become with their writing.

FORMAL WRITING PRACTICE 1 (page 67)

| Answers may vary.

FORMAL WRITING PRACTICE 2 (page 67)

| Answers may vary.

Formal Writing: *Persuasive Essay* (page 67)

One of the most common types of writing that students are called upon to produce is the persuasive essay. Yet this type of essay is daunting for students who have had little experience taking a position on a controversial issue and then arguing it through in writing by presenting evidence, including the opinions of others. Some teachers prepare students to argue persuasively by having them practice in oral class debates. Students can use the actual essay topics they will write about (see the choices on page 67), or they can practice using other topics.

If you choose to use oral debates, divide the class in half or into smaller teams. Each team should come up with an agreed upon number of examples of evidence to support their point. Tell them to include both evidence in favor of their position and evidence showing why the opposition's position is wrong. Working in a group and having the opportunity to present evidence as a group – with each person presenting one idea, for example – makes the process easier than if each student had to develop and present an entire argument on his or her own.

Regardless of whether you choose to use oral debates, be sure to discuss with your students the techniques for organizing persuasive essays presented in the second paragraph of this section on page 67.

Getting Started: *Asking and Answering Questions* (page 68)

Point out to students that this activity leads them through a step-by-step analysis of their argument and that the steps described will serve them well in preparing to write any persuasive essay.

REVISING (pages 68–70)

See page ix of this manual for teaching guidelines about revising.

In analyzing the essay on pages 69–70, students should discuss the following questions: What are the strongest points in the argument? Are there weak points? What makes these points strong or weak? Then they should look carefully at the conclusion and decide if it serves any of the purposes listed on page 66 and whether it is effective. Elicit from students the fact that this writer states his opinion clearly in the introduction and then gives examples. Note that this is the opposite of the approach taken by Sunita Puri in "Cultural Identity vs. Ethnic Fashions." Puri presents examples first and then states her position in the conclusion.

EDITING (pages 70–78)

See page x of this manual for teaching guidelines about editing.

Grammar: *Articles* (pages 71–74)

One of the biggest problems that learners of English face is articles. The rules for articles are quite arbitrary and often differ from the student's first or other languages. One particularly difficult aspect of articles is the concept of countable and uncountable nouns. Students usually do best by memorizing the rules and then testing out what they have memorized by looking at newspapers, magazines, and books to see how articles are actually used by professional writers. They enjoy finding exceptions to rules and sometimes these exceptions help them to understand the rules better.

GRAMMAR PRACTICE 1 (page 73)

1 *The* teacher told us *the* name of every student in (optional *the*) class on *the* first day of school.

2 Each of *the* students got together with one other student to do *the* interview.

3 We asked for each other's names, how long we had been in (optional *the*) college, how long we had been in *the* country, and how long we had spoken English.

4 *A* classmate told me about *the* problems he had eating in school. He hated *the* coffee in *the* cafeteria and complained that *the* food wasn't as good as *the* food he had at home.

GRAMMAR PRACTICE 2 (page 74)

Answers may vary.

GRAMMAR PRACTICE 3 (page 74)

See *Answer Key* in Student's Book, pages 237–238.

Mechanics: *Plurals* (page 74–78)

As with articles, students usually have to memorize the rules for plurals.

MECHANICS PRACTICE 1 (page 77)

See *Answer Key* in Student's Book, page 238.

MECHANICS PRACTICE 2 (page 78)

See *Answer Key* in Student's Book, page 238.

Chapter Five

A GLOBAL ANALYSIS OF CULTURE

"A Global Analysis of Culture" is taken from sociologist Alex Thio's textbook *Sociology: A Brief Introduction.* Using a structure common to many textbooks that students encounter, Thio focuses on culture: cultural universals, culture clashes, ethnocentrism, and cultural relativism.

PREREADING (pages 79–80)

See page vi of this manual for teaching guidelines about prereading and reading.

In this chapter, you may want to begin by having students discuss the questions on page 79 before they discuss the illustration. Then ask them what the illustration evokes about cultures around the world.

The vocabulary task on page 80 presents passages taken from the text. Students should attempt to figure out the meaning of the italicized words from the context. If they cannot, they should feel free to use the dictionary. It is important, however, that students practice explaining the meaning of each passage in their own words.

POSTREADING (pages 84–85)

See page vii of this manual for teaching guidelines about postreading.

Think about the Content (page 84)

1 According to Thio, the main reason for the most violent conflicts between societies has been cultural and linguistic differences. (Par. 6)

2 *Ethnocentrism* is the attitude that one's own culture is superior to that of other peoples. (Par. 11) Answers to the rest of the question may vary.

3 *Cultural relativism* is the belief that a culture must be understood on its own terms. (Par. 14) When President Clinton tried to view the situation with China from a different perspective, one more culturally attuned to the perspective of the Chinese themselves, he stopped pressuring China on human rights issues and focused on trade issues. He was then accused of giving up on improving human rights issues in China. (Pars. 16–17)

4 Answers may vary.

Think about the Writing (pages 84–85)

1 Thio asks two questions in the introductory paragraph: "But are cultures universally the same in some ways?" and "Do cultural differences cause international conflict and violence?" He answers the first question in paragraphs 2–3 by giving examples of some of the ways in which cultures are the same: the development of some kind of food-getting technology, the construction of some kind of shelter, the creation of some means of communication, and the creation of art forms and belief systems. He answers the second question in paragraphs 5–9. In paragraph 5, he says:

> The differences among these cultural domains [civilizations] can be expected to generate most of the conflict around the globe. As Huntington (1996) observes, in the new world emerging from the ashes of the cold war, the dominating source of international

conflict will no longer be political or economic but instead cultural. Huntington offers a number of reasons, including the following.

Paragraphs 6–9 give examples of Huntington's reasons.

2 Answers may vary.

3 "Culture Clash" is a little essay within a larger article. It contains an introduction, is organized by enumerating points – first, second, third, and fourth – and ends with a concluding paragraph. The main idea of the "Culture Clash" section is found in its conclusion (Par. 10): ". . . culture clash may create more conflict and violence in the world. This may not happen if people learn to understand each other's cultures, especially in the ways people in a different culture see their own interests."

4 Answers may vary.

A Personal Response (page 85)

Answers may vary.

WRITING (pages 85–87)

See page viii of this manual for teaching guidelines about writing.

Journal Writing (page 85)

Remind students to use their journals as a place to reflect and think without worrying about spelling, grammar, or the mechanics of writing.

Formal Writing: *Paraphrasing* (pages 85–86)

Paraphrasing is one of the most challenging skills for students to develop and one of the most necessary ones for academic writing. *Formal Writing Practice* on page 86 asks students to decide which of two paraphrases is acceptable and which is not. After eliciting the answers (the first one is acceptable; the second one is not), have students refer to the paraphrasing guidelines on pages 85–86 to explain the reasons for their answers.

Most students will need to practice paraphrasing repeatedly before they feel comfortable paraphrasing in their writing. You can take other passages from the Thio reading or from any other reading in the book and ask students to practice paraphrasing them. In some classes, it works best when students do this with a partner or in a small group for the first few times. As they become more competent, they can do it on their own. Then they need practice learning how to include and cite paraphrased material in their writing. Learning this will be an ongoing process for them as they write the remaining assignments in this book as well as papers for other college courses.

Paraphrase 1 is acceptable because it restates the ideas of the source in quite different words, is about the same length as the original, and clearly states the source. The passage quoted from the original is not too long and is placed within quotation marks. Paraphrase 2 is not acceptable because it is longer than the original, does not state the source, and merely substitutes synonyms for the words in the original.

Formal Writing: *Writing a Summary* (pages 86–87)

Most students are asked to write summaries of material they have read in a wide variety of courses. The point of having them write essay-length, one-paragraph, and one-sentence summaries is that there is no correct, set length for a summary: Summaries can be long or short, detailed or not, depending on their purpose. Therefore, it is useful for students to practice writing summaries of varying lengths and to be aware of different purposes and audiences when writing a summary.

After students do the writing assignment on page 87, you may want to assign a summary of material from one of their other college texts as additional practice. Since you will probably not be familiar with the text, ask your students to photocopy the page or pages they are summarizing.

Getting Started: *Taking Notes on a Text* (pages 88–89)

An essential prerequisite to writing a summary is taking good notes on what one has read (or heard – as in a summary of a lecture). After students have performed the two steps in this activity, you may want them to take notes from which they could write a summary based on a text they are using in another course. If you have students do this, be sure they provide a photocopy of the text for you along with their notes.

REVISING (pages 89–91)

See page ix of this manual for teaching guidelines about revising.

The activity provided in *Analyze Other People's Writing* gives students additional experience analyzing summaries. If your students wrote summaries based on material from other courses, as suggested above, you can also ask them to analyze those summaries using the analysis questions in this activity.

EDITING (pages 91–97)

See page x of this manual for teaching guidelines about editing.

Grammar: *The Passive Voice* (pages 91–95)

Understanding what the passive voice is and how it is formed is necessary for students who are reading academic texts and writing academic papers.

Although we usually encourage students to use the active rather than passive voice in their writing, there is a place for the passive voice, especially in academic writing, and students need to know how to use it effectively.

GRAMMAR PRACTICE 1 (pages 92–93)

1 After her concert, Madonna was surrounded by fans.
2 The new wing of the Louvre museum was designed by I. M. Pei.
3 Rice is grown in Southeast Asia.
4 The DNA sample is being analyzed by the laboratory.
5 My blood was drawn yesterday by a medical technician.
6 *The Lord of the Rings* trilogy was directed by Peter Jackson.
7 The figures at Stonehenge have been studied by many scholars.

GRAMMAR PRACTICE 2 (page 93)

1 **P** = passive; **A** = active
   Note that in some cases the active sentence must be changed slightly to make sense. In these cases, variations on the answers below are possible.

   • **P** Some [needs], such as the need for food and shelter, are rooted in biology. (Par. 1)
     A Biology is the root of some of our needs, such as food and shelter.

   • **P** For example, religion is a cultural universal, but its specific content varies from one culture to another, as can be seen in the differences among Christianity, Islam, Judaism, Confucianism, and so on. (Par. 4)
     A . . . as Christianity, Islam, Judaism, Confucianism show us.

   • **P** These cultures can be classified into larger groupings called *cultural domains,* popularly known as *civilizations.* (Par. 4)
     A *Civilization* is the word that describes the classification of cultures into larger groupings, or *cultural domains.*

   • **P** The differences among these cultural domains can be expected to generate most of the conflict around the globe. (Par. 5)
     A Most conflict around the globe will occur because of the differences among these cultural domains.

   • **P** These differences do not necessarily mean conflict or violence, as can be proven by the increasing appearance of multiple languages on the Internet. (Par. 6)
     A The increasing appearance of multiple languages on the Internet proves that these differences do not necessarily mean conflict or violence.

   • **P** Almost from the time we are born, we are taught that our way of life is good, moral, civilized, or natural. (Par. 11)
     A Almost from the time we are born, we learn that our way of life is . . .

- **P** Although ethnocentrism is universal, it <u>can be suppressed</u> with cultural relativism . . . (Par. 14)
  A Cultural relativism can suppress the universal sense of ethnocentrism . . .

- **P** In our legalistic, rule-oriented culture, a written contract <u>is usually required</u> for conducting business. (Par. 15)
  A To conduct business in our legalistic, rule-oriented culture, you usually need to have a written contract.

- **P** Once a contract <u>is signed</u>, negotiations should more or less cease. (Par. 15)
  A Negotiations should more or less cease, once you sign a contract.

- **P** The contract is only a charter for serious negotiations, which will stop only after the work <u>is completed</u>. (Par. 15)
  A . . . , which will stop only after the work's completion.

- **P** But Clinton <u>was criticized</u> for kowtowing to China by ignoring its human rights abuses. (Par. 17)
  A People criticized Clinton for kowtowing to China by ignoring its human rights abuses.

- **P** This raises the question of how far cultural relativism <u>should be carried</u>. (Par. 17)
  A This raises the question of how far we should carry cultural relativism.

- **P** <u>Should</u> ethical judgment <u>be suspended</u> when others engage in such horrors as infanticide, genital mutilation, torture, or genocide? (Par. 17)
  A Should people suspend ethical judgment when others engage in such horrors as . . .

2 Answers may vary.

GRAMMAR PRACTICE 3 (page 94)

See *Answer Key* in Student's Book, page 238.

GRAMMAR PRACTICE 4 (page 94)

See *Answer Key* in Student's Book, page 239.

Mechanics: *Commas* (pages 95–97)

One of the most difficult punctuation challenges for writers of English is the comma. We use them more than any other punctuation mark, and we have many rules that govern their use. Once students have reviewed the rules and done some of the practices, they should look at other texts they have read and written to analyze how and why the commas were used. It can also be a helpful experience for students to find mistakes in professional writing. As a class, you can discuss whether the mistakes are stylistic, intentional, or appear to be careless editing. Students need to realize that there is some flexibility in rules (and also that in some cases there is not).

MECHANICS PRACTICE 1 (page 96)

1 Food, shelter, and companionship [items in a series] are some of the primary reasons why people live in societies.

2 Companionship, which means so much to most of us, [information that if omitted would still leave a complete and meaningful sentence] is not always included in the list of important aspects of human life, [comma required before coordinating conjunction, *but*] but I think it really matters.

3 Even though some of these needs may be met by a person living alone, [introductory dependent clause] most people agree that it is more satisfying to live with others.

4 My neighbor, Harold Crystal, [appositive noun] has lived in the same house since he was born, [comma required before coordinating conjunction, *and*] and now that his parents are gone, [introductory dependent clause] he lives there with his wife and children.

5 Generally, [transitional expression] most people move at least three times during their lives, [comma required before coordinating conjunction, *so*] so my neighbor is unusual.

6 The stability of a neighborhood like mine, therefore, [commas required around transitional expression, *therefore,* because it is in the middle of a sentence] is because of people like Harold Crystal.

MECHANICS PRACTICE 2 (page 97)

See *Answer Key* in Student's Book, page 239.

Chapter Six

THE ALL-AMERICAN SLURP

"The All-American Slurp" is a short story by Lensey Chao Namioka that tells about cultural differences and their resolutions through the story of two families – an immigrant family newly arrived from China and a native-born United States family.

PREREADING (pages 98–99)

See page vi of this manual for teaching guidelines about prereading and reading.

Ask students to look at the illustration on page 98 and discuss how the title of the story is reflected in what the two girls are doing. What is a slurp? When do people slurp food? Is it considered polite to do this in any culture? Then discuss the questions on page 98 with the class.

The vocabulary task on page 99 presents passages taken from the story. Students should attempt to figure out the meaning of the italicized words in the passages from the context. If they cannot, they should feel free to use the dictionary. It is important, however, that students practice explaining the meaning of each passage in their own words.

POSTREADING (pages 106–107)

See page vii of this manual for teaching guidelines about postreading.

Think about the Content (page 106)

1 The Lins:
   The Lins are not used to eating raw vegetables; celery is especially challenging because it can be stringy. (Pars. 1, 9, 10) The Lins do not usually eat dairy products. (Par. 5) They are also unaccustomed to buffet-style service, where people fill their plates from a table and then sit and eat with their plates in their laps. (Pars. 12, 14) The Lins order soup in a French restaurant and tilt their soup plates to drink it, slurping loudly enough to attract the attention of other diners. (Pars. 41–46)

   The Gleasons:
   When the Gleasons are invited to dinner at the Lins, they take food from each serving dish, mix it together, and eat it all at once. This horrifies the Lins, who are used to taking a small amount of one type of food, eating it, then taking a small portion of a different food, and so on. The Gleasons are also clumsy with chopsticks. (Pars. 58–59)

2 Meg and the other girls in school wear jeans and T-shirts, but the narrator wears blouses, skirts, and dresses. The narrator has Chinese dresses with high collars and slits up the sides, which she allows Meg to try on. [It could be interesting to discuss why Meg's wearing this dress leads her to strike "several sultry poses" until the two girls "nearly fell over laughing."] The narrator's family does not have a car at the beginning of the story, but the Gleason family does have one. The narrator does not have her own bike and has to borrow one from a neighbor. The narrator's family has different furniture from the neighbors and ends up buying "all the furniture we needed, plus a dart board and a 1,000-piece jigsaw puzzle" at a rummage sale. [You might ask students why they think the author reveals that the jigsaw puzzle is missing a piece.] (Pars. 22, 28–29) The mother is not used

to wearing high heels but wears them to go to a parent-teacher conference. At the conference, following the Chinese custom of not bragging about your children, the Lins tell the teacher that their daughter is "a very stupid girl" and that "the teacher was showing favoritism toward [her]." (Par. 53)

3 Answers may vary.

Think about the Writing (pages 106–107)

1–3 Answers may vary.

4 The past perfect is used to indicate that one past event occurred before another mentioned later in the sentence or paragraph. Par. 1: *had emigrated*; Par. 2: *had been invited* (past perfect passive); Par. 18: *had both studied* and *had studied*; Par. 33: *had eaten*; Par. 42: *had studied*; Par. 53: *had been*; Par. 54: *had invited*; Par. 58: *had been taking* (past perfect progressive)

Every time there is dialogue between characters, the present tense is used.

When Namioka wants to show a habitual action or general sense of time, she uses the present tense.

Par. 5: Most Chinese *don't* care for dairy products . . .

Par. 9: When I *help* my mother in the kitchen, I always *pull* the strings out before slicing celery.

Par. 16: My mother also *puts* everything on the table and *hopes* for the best.

Par. 43: As any respectable Chinese *knows*, the correct way to eat your soup *is* to slurp. This *helps* to cool the liquid and *prevents* you from burning your lips. It also *shows* your appreciation.

Par. 45: You *know* how it *sounds* on a rocky beach when the tide *goes* out and the water *drains* from all those little pools? They go *shloop, shloop, shloop.*

Par. 51: A girl *can't leave* her family just because they *slurp* their soup.

Par. 52: Even now, I *turn* hot all over when I *think* of the Lakeview restaurant.

A Personal Response (page 107)

Answers may vary.

WRITING (pages 107–108)

See page viii of this manual for teaching guidelines about writing.

Journal Writing (page 107)

Remind students to use their journals as a place to reflect and think without worrying about spelling, grammar, or the mechanics of writing.

Formal Writing: *Narration, or Telling a Story* (pages 107–108)

Many students like to tell stories, both orally and in writing. Point out to them that storytelling (narration) is the basis of most writing, whether nonfiction or fiction. Discuss how the essays they have written so far in working with this book have all included narration.

In this chapter, students are given the option of writing either a nonfiction narrative or a short story. Though they are not writing a conventional academic essay, they should keep in mind the fact that they still need an introduction (a beginning), a middle (development), and an end (a conclusion). They should also be thinking about the narration as a vehicle that leads them toward a main idea or understanding about something (as the Namioka story does). Remind them that direct speech or dialogue usually requires the present tense while the narration of a story usually relies on a variety of past tenses.

Getting Started: *Brainstorming* (pages 108–109)

You might want to have students read "The Two Mosquito Bites," the essay in the *Revising* section, prior to brainstorming. (See *Revising*, immediately below.) Brainstorming is a good technique for students to use as they think about a story they want to tell. They can work alone, with a partner, or in a small group. Many students prefer to begin the process alone and then get feedback from a partner or a small group.

REVISING (pages 109–111)

See page ix of this manual for teaching guidelines about revising.

"The Two Mosquito Bites" is fun for students to read and analyze. It may be a good idea to do this activity before the brainstorming activity in *Getting Started* because the story may give them ideas about traditions and superstitions that could lead to interesting narratives.

EDITING (pages 111–116)

See page x of this manual for teaching guidelines about editing.

Grammar: *Sentence Variety* (pages 111–115)

As students become better able to express themselves in writing, they are ready to begin to look at style and variety. In this chapter, they learn that their writing can become more complex, interesting, and subtle, if they vary the types of sentences they use. Encourage students to experiment with the different sentence types in their writing.

GRAMMAR PRACTICE 1 (page 112)

Answers may vary.

GRAMMAR PRACTICE 2 (page 112)

Answers may vary.

GRAMMAR PRACTICE 3 (page 113)

Answers may vary. Here are some possible answers.

1 The Lin family enjoyed eating at home, and they enjoyed eating in restaurants.

2 The Lin family went to an elegant French restaurant, so they could celebrate Mr. Lin's promotion.

3 Mrs. Lin was a good cook, but she was was not sure if everyone would like her food.

4 Many people like to try new foods, so cooks create new recipes with interesting ingredients.

5 She could make dinner for her friends, or she could invite them to a restaurant.

GRAMMAR PRACTICE 4 (page 114)

Answers may vary. Here are some possible answers.

1 When people are hesitant to try unfamiliar foods, they often order the same dishes in restaurants.
People often order the same dishes in restaurants if they are hesitant to try unfamiliar foods.
People often order the same dishes in restaurants because they are hesitant to try unfamiliar foods.

2 When the Lins had western guests, they set the table with large dinner plates.
The Lins set the table with large dinner plates since they had western guests.

3 Because many western people are not comfortable with chopsticks, Asian restaurants have forks and knives for them.
If western people are not comfortable with chopsticks, Asian restaurants have forks and knives for them.
Asian restaurants have forks and knives since many western people are not comfortable with chopsticks.

4 The Lins were shocked when the Gleasons put rice, prawns, chicken, meat, and sauce on their plates all at once.
   When the Gleasons put rice, prawns, chicken, meat, and sauce on their plates all at once, the Lins were shocked.

5 Although the narrator of the story seems out of place at first, she later makes a good friend and learns to accept her family.
   The narrator of the story seems out of place at first even though in the end she makes a good friend and learns to accept her family.

GRAMMAR PRACTICE 5 (page 114)

See *Answer Key* in Student's Book, page 240.

Mechanics: *Punctuating Direct Speech* (pages 115–116)

The ability to punctuate direct speech is important in many types of writing. In academic writing, for example, direct speech can be used to report information from an interview or a lecture. Thus, the correct punctuation of direct speech is an important skill for students to master. Once they have done the exercises in the book, they can examine readings from other sources to see how direct speech is punctuated. They may come across examples where writers have broken the rules of punctuation. This is a good place to discuss the different expectations for professional (especially fiction) writers and student writers. Student writers must show that they know the rules before they are permitted to break or challenge them.

MECHANICS PRACTICE 1 (page 115)

Answers may vary.

MECHANICS PRACTICE 2 (page 115)

Answers may vary.

MECHANICS PRACTICE 3 (page 116)

See *Answer Key* in Student's Book, page 240.

UNIT THREE
Work

Chapter Seven
....
AGE AND YOUTH

In Chapter 7, the reading is "Age and Youth," a personal essay written by Pablo Casals at the age of 93. Casals finds inspiration both in his music and his natural environment; his optimism and joy in living pervade the essay.

PREREADING (pages 118–119)

See page vi of this manual for teaching guidelines about prereading and reading.

Ask students to look at the illustration on page 118 and describe the details they observe. What is the setting? What musical instruments are shown? What do students think the selection that follows will be about? Then discuss the questions on page 118 with the class.

The vocabulary task on page 119 presents passages taken from the text. Students should attempt to figure out the meaning of the italicized sections in the passages from the context. If they cannot, they should feel free to use the dictionary. It is important, however, that students practice explaining the meaning of each passage in their own words.

POSTREADING (pages 121–122)

See page vii of this manual for teaching guidelines about postreading.

Think about the Content (page 121)

Answers may vary. Here are some possible answers.

1 Casals has a positive attitude toward life, a zest for life. He still lives fully, despite his age. He has a good sense of humor as evidenced by his response to the letter from his friend. He gets great joy from his music and from nature.

2 Casals rejects the concept of retirement. He sees his work as his life. He writes, "Work and interest in worthwhile things are the best remedy for age." (Par. 5) As a result, he continues to be an active musician.

3 In Paragraph 7 Casals discusses his "amazement at the miracle of nature." He lives by the sea because he finds it fascinating and loves to walk along its shores every morning. The sea is "infinitely variable . . . always becoming something different and new."

Think about the Writing (page 121)

Answers may vary. Here are some possible answers.

1 He includes the letter so that the reader will go through the process of thinking what the letter proposes is real and then finding out that it is a joke. Furthermore, just telling about the letter would not convey its flavor.

2 Casals' opening sentence captures the reader's interest; it is unusual to read an essay by a person who is 93 years old. The thesis statement is sentence 5: "If you continue to work and to absorb the beauty in the world about you, you find that age does not necessarily mean getting old." The conclusion restates the thesis statement in a metaphorical way. Casals talks about the sea and its beauty. He implies that looking at the sea provides him with the sense of the beauty and infinite mystery of life. Students will probably find both the introduction and the conclusion effective.

3 Casals describes his morning routine to show how active he is, how ordered his day is, and how his routine adds to his appreciation of every day of his life. Students will probably find it effective.

A Personal Response (page 122)

Answers may vary.

WRITING (pages 122–123)

See page viii of this manual for teaching guidelines about writing.

Journal Writing (page 122)

Remind students to use their journals as a place to reflect and think without worrying about spelling, grammar, or the mechanics of writing.

Formal Writing: *Descriptive Essay* (pages 122–123)

When responding to student writing, teachers often say "Add more details," and students may not know how to go about doing this. In this assignment, they are given the opportunity to work specifically on this skill by describing a person, a place, or an object. Many teachers ask students to do all three in order to give them the chance to think about how each subject requires different language. Make sure students understand that they should not just write a long list of details; rather, they must find ways to communicate why the subject of their essay is important to them.

Getting Started: *Making Quadrants* (page 123)

This technique works very well with visually oriented students. It is also good for those students who are more comfortable thinking about parts or details rather than seeing the whole essay holistically.

REVISING (pages 124–125)

See page ix of this manual for teaching guidelines about revising.

Students often enjoy "Memories of Papa Victor" so much that they have difficulty coming up with suggestions for change. You might point out the interesting way Ortiz describes his grandfather: "He was a man with the body shape of a black bear and the heart of a nun." After students discuss what this means, ask if they would have preferred a more literal physical description of the man – his height, weight, coloring, hair type, etc. Why do they think the writer included so many details of place in telling about a person? What other details would they like to know?

EDITING (pages 125–130)

See page x of this manual for teaching guidelines about editing.

Grammar: *Using Prepositions* (pages 126–130)

Next to the use of articles, the use of prepositions is one of the most challenging aspects of learning English. At one time, English relied on inflectional endings to explain relationships among elements in a sentence. Today English has very few inflectional endings (*-ed, -s, -ing, -er, -est*) and relies instead on prepositions to establish relationships. As a result, the subtle nuances in meaning of prepositions present a challenge. In this chapter, some of the basic rules are presented. Much of what students will need to know about prepositions will come with time and reading.

GRAMMAR PRACTICE 1 (page 129)

1 *at*; *in*; *on*
2 *at*; *in*
3 *to*; *in*
4 *at*; *in*
5 *in*; *in*; *on*; *at*; *in*
6 *in*; *on*; *on*
7 *for*; *with* (or *at*); *at*

8 *by*; *to*
9 *for*; *on*
10 *on*; *before*; *after*
11 *in*; *in*; *on*; *in*; *on*
12 *in*; *on*
13 *in*; *at*; *in*

GRAMMAR PRACTICE 2 (page 130)

Answers may vary.

GRAMMAR PRACTICE 3 (page 130)

| See *Answer Key* in Student's Book, page 240.

Mechanics: *Run-On Sentences and Comma Splices* (pages 131–132)

A significant part of becoming a better writer is learning how to analyze your own writing to locate and correct your own errors. Learning how to recognize run-on sentences and comma splices is hard for some students because we often talk with words and ideas that run together and overlap. One trick that sometimes helps students is to read backwards, noting where sentences begin and end. Another trick is to read aloud, paying attention to where your voice drops – does this indicate a comma (a brief pause) or a period (a longer pause)?

MECHANICS PRACTICE 1 (pages 131–132)

Answers may vary. Here are some sample answers.

1 Because Pablo Casals always loved music, he learned to play the cello.
Pablo Casals always loved music; he learned to play the cello.
Pablo Casals always loved music, so he learned to play the cello.
Pablo Casals, who always loved music, learned to play the cello.

2 His friend Sasha Schneider played a joke on him, and Schneider sent Casals a letter inviting him to conduct an orchestra.
His friend Sasha Schneider played a joke on him; Schneider sent Casals a letter inviting him to conduct an orchestra.
His friend Sasha Schneider played a joke on him when Schneider sent Casals a letter inviting him to conduct an orchestra.

3 Casals liked to live near the sea, and he enjoyed early morning walks on the beach.
Casals liked to live near the sea; he enjoyed early morning walks on the beach.
Casals liked to live near the sea where he enjoyed early morning walks on the beach.
Because Cassals enjoyed early morning walks on the beach, he liked to live near the sea.
Casals, who liked to live near the sea, enjoyed early morning walks on the beach.

4 Looking at nature made Casals very happy, and he felt connected to life in that way.
Looking at nature made Casals very happy; he felt connected to life in that way.
Looking at nature made Casals very happy because he felt connected to life in that way.
Casals felt happy looking at nature, which made him feel connected to life.

5 Some elderly people continue to work and absorb beauty around them, so they feel that aging does not mean getting old.

Some elderly people continue to work and absorb beauty around them; they feel that aging does not mean getting old.

Because some elderly people continue to work and absorb beauty around them, they feel that aging does not mean getting old.

Elderly people who continue to work and absorb beauty around them feel that aging does not mean getting old.

For some elderly people, if they continue to work and absorb beauty around them, they feel that aging does not mean getting old.

MECHANICS PRACTICE **2** (page 132)

See *Answer Key* in Student's Book, page 241.

Chapter Eight

JOB SATISFACTION

"Job Satisfaction," by Stephen P. Robbins, is an academic essay excerpted from a textbook on organizational behavior. The essay deals with the qualities that affect personal attitudes toward one's work experience.

PREREADING (pages 133–134)

See page vi of this manual for teaching guidelines about prereading and reading.

Ask your students to look at the illustration on page 133 and discuss what jobs are depicted. Then discuss the questions on page 133 with the class.

The vocabulary task on page 134 presents passages taken from the text. Students should attempt to figure out the meaning of the italicized sections in the passages from the context. If they cannot, they should feel free to use the dictionary. It is important, however, that students practice explaining the meaning of each passage in their own words.

POSTREADING (pages 137–138)

See page vii of this manual for teaching guidelines about postreading.

Think about the Content (page 137)

1 People prefer jobs that provide opportunities to use their intelligence and skills as well as those that offer them a chance to perform a variety of

tasks. People want jobs that stimulate them, so they do not get bored on the job. However, they also do not want to be so challenged that they are frustrated and fear failure. (Par. 3) You might want to ask your students to compare two different jobs in relation to mental challenge: a teacher and an accountant, a doctor and a lawyer, a nurse and a detective, for example.

2 Pay is always a tricky subject. People usually think pay is fair when it is ". . . based on job demands, individual skill level, and community pay standards. . . . But the key in linking pay to satisfaction is not the absolute amount one is paid; rather, it is the perception of fairness." People also want promotion polices that are "fair and just." (Par. 4) It is interesting that some people are willing to accept lower pay to work in a better location, in a less demanding job, or to have greater independence in their work and in the hours they work. You might ask your students to discuss what matters more to them and why – higher pay or better working conditions.

3 Answers may vary.

Think about the Writing (pages 137–138)

1 In paragraph 2, Robbins tells his readers what the essay will be about. At this point, you might ask students to review introductions (pages 47–48 in the Student's Book) and decide which technique(s) Robbins uses.

2 Answers may vary.

3 Answers may vary. Here are some possible answers.
Robbins's writing is not exciting, but it is clear and is designed to be useful to college students. First, he defines his terms throughout, beginning in the first sentence: "Job satisfaction [refers to] an individual's general attitude toward his or her job." He asks questions and answers them as seen in paragraph 2: "What work-related variables determine job satisfaction? An extensive review of the literature indicates that the more important factors . . . include mentally challenging work, equitable rewards, supportive working conditions, and supportive colleagues." Robbins uses intellectually challenging vocabulary – vocabulary that is appropriate for college students and that may be used in other psychology or sociology classes – such as *inherent, assessment, complex summation, factors, conducive,* and *equitable.* Learning and using this vocabulary is important for students who are building their academic writing skills. Next, he divides the article into sections that make it easier for the reader to understand the different categories covered in the article.

A Personal Response (page 138)

Answers may vary.

WRITING (pages 138–141)

See page viii of this manual for teaching guidelines about writing.

Journal Writing (page 138)

Remind students to use their journals as a place to reflect and think without worrying about spelling, grammar, or the mechanics of writing.

Formal Writing: *Writing a Persuasive Essay Under Test Conditions* (pages 138–141)

In many programs, students are required to write an essay for the purpose of placing them in the correct level; at the end of the semester, they are required to take another essay exam to demonstrate whether they are ready to move to the following level. Such essay exams are usually timed and often students receive the topics at the time of the exam.

A common type of essay exam requires students to take a position on an issue, argue the position with at least three reasons or examples to support their position, and have both an effective introduction and conclusion. The set time period is often an hour. An important aspect of this type of exam is that either choice is correct; what matters is how well students develop their essays. Most students find this challenging, particularly students for whom English is not their first language. In this chapter, students are introduced to strategies that will help them take this type of exam, and then they practice those strategies in a simulated test.

As part of the simulated test, students are required to make an outline (the *Getting Started* activity) and revise and edit their papers. Therefore, before you begin to prepare your students for the simulated test, be sure that you have read all the instructions on *Formal Writing* in the Student's Book, including the *Writing Assignment* on page 141. Then finish reading this section. After you have read this section, read the sections on *Revising* and *Editing*, below.

Be sure to give students enough time to read and discuss the sample question and sample responses on pages 139–140. I also recommend that you (or a student) read aloud the test-taking strategies on page 141 and then discuss them as a class. You might want to suggest that students copy them onto a 4 × 6 card or small piece of paper to keep with them while they take the test. Of course, you could write the strategies on the board during the practice test, but copying them will help students internalize them. If you have students write out the strategies, point out that this is a step in helping them remember the strategies, since they would probably not be allowed to bring any paper into an actual exam.

Outlining is an essential skill that students should know how to use, so be sure that all students use this method of getting started for the practice test. In fact, you might want to collect their outlines together with their essays. It is very important that you have students practice outlining Sample Essay 2,

CHAPTER 8 *Job Satisfaction* **39**

which they are instructed to do in *Getting Started*, on pages 141–142, *before* they take the "test." Consider collecting the outlines of Sample Essay 2, photocopying a few of the good ones, and distributing them for the class to discuss. You can also give the class one or two outlines that need improvement and elicit how they could be improved.

Students may very well have looked ahead and seen the test questions. So, if you would like to substitute others, three more questions are provided below. Another possibility is to let students take the test in the book as "practice," and follow it up at a later date with a second test in which you give them a choice of two of these questions or two questions of your own.

> Your community has a budget problem and must make a decision about where to cut costs that will cause everyone the least harm. One possibility is to eliminate free bus transfers and charge an additional fare to anyone who needs to transfer. The other choice is to eliminate free borrowing of books and videos from neighborhood libraries and charge a small fee of $1.00 for every book and/or video that is borrowed from the library. Which choice would you make and why?

> Your school would like to offer a new technology service to all students. One possibility is to offer free laptop computers to all full-time students. The other possibility is to provide free fast Internet connections to all students either in their dorm rooms or in their homes. Which do you think would be better for the students in your school and why?

> The Language Center in your college would like to offer extra support to all students studying a language. They are trying to decide whether to provide free tapes or videos to students to use for the semester or one hour of free one-to-one tutoring each week. Which do you think is the better choice and why?

Getting Started: *Outlining* (pages 141–142)
See *Formal Writing* (above).

REVISING (pages 142–143)
See page ix of this manual for teaching guidelines about revising.

You may either collect the practice tests immediately or choose to let students practice revising their practice tests in a more leisurely way. If you give them a second test later, you could let them have a second chance at revising this first one with a partner but not allow them to revise after the fact in the second test.

EDITING (pages 143–149)

See page x of this manual for teaching guidelines about editing.

In the simulated test students take, they have to check their grammar and mechanics but are not told to look for any specific kinds of errors. After they do the work on relative clauses, you may want them to review their test essays to see if they have errors regarding these. Another possibility is to have students review one or two of their other essays – or an essay for another class – to check for the proper use of relative clauses. You can follow the same procedure for the *Mechanics* section.

Grammar: *Relative Clauses* (pages 143–147)

Because they are concerned about making mistakes, students may not use relative clauses. This is especially true when it comes to taking essay exams. Students frequently stick with the tried and true. However, adding some variety to their essays by using relative clauses can make their essays stronger and more effective.

GRAMMAR PRACTICE 1 (page 145)

1 *that can be used for only one purpose* (restrictive adjective clause)
2 *that were considered* (restrictive adjective clause)
3 *that will benefit all the employees* (restrictive adjective clause)
4 *who was working as a babysitter at that time* (nonrestrictive adjective clause)
5 *where they can go* (nonrestrictive adverbial clause)

GRAMMAR PRACTICE 2 (pages 145–146)

1 *that* (restrictive adjective clause)

2 *that / in which* (restrictive adjective clause)

3 *, who* (nonrestrictive adjective clause; a comma must be added after *night* to indicate the end of the clause)

4 *, whose* (nonrestrictive adjective clause; a comma must be added after *year* to indicate the end of the clause)

5 *, which* (nonrestrictive adjective clause)
(Point out to students that when using *which* in a nonrestrictive adjective clause, it should be preceded by a comma. If the sentence read "She takes classes at *the* Yoga for You which is on Main Street," it would be a restrictive adjective clause and would not take a comma.)

6 *where* (restrictive adverbial clause)

Answers may vary. Here are some possible answers.

2 Helene, who sent out many job application letters, received only one reply.
  Helene, who received only one reply, sent out many job application letters.

3 She went for an interview in an office that was on the top floor of a tall building.

4 The interviewer, who was friendly and smart, asked some tough questions.

5 Helene was offered the job she wanted, which was an entry-level position in the company.

6 She will be working for several of the people whom she met during the interview.

GRAMMAR PRACTICE 4 (page 146)

Answers may vary.

GRAMMAR PRACTICE 5 (pages 146–147)

See *Answer Key* in Student's Book, page 241.

Mechanics: *Fragments* (pages 147–149)

Being able to identify and correct fragments is important, especially for students taking timed essay exams in which they must write quickly. Reading backwards is a good trick to help locate fragments. With experience, students become aware that attaching a hanging fragment to the independent clause that preceded or followed will help to form a complete sentence.

Students often notice fragments in professional writing, especially in literary forms. Remind students that professional writers are allowed the freedom to experiment with language and form because they know the rules and can apply them when necessary, but students are expected to demonstrate that they know the rules in their writing.

MECHANICS PRACTICE 1 (page 148)

Numbers 2, 4, and 5 are complete sentences.
Here are some possible ways to correct the fragments:

When I finish this class, I will understand more English.

Because she studied hard, she got an A.

He quit because the work was strenuous.

You might want to encourage your students to try correcting the fragments with additional words of their own.

MECHANICS PRACTICE 2 (page 149)

See *Answer Key* in Student's Book, page 241.

Chapter Nine

VILLAGE IS MORE GLOBAL, LANGUAGE IS MORE VITAL

"Village Is More Global, Language Is More Vital" is a newspaper article by Marcin Skomial that discusses the advantages of multilingualism in the workplace of today.

PREREADING (pages 150–151)

See page vi of this manual for teaching guidelines about prereading and reading.

Begin by discussing the illustration on page 150, which shows a woman looking at the classified ads in a newspaper. Students can discuss their own techniques for finding a job: Some may use newspaper ads, some may use Internet job lists, some may ask friends or other contacts, some use personnel agencies, and some rely on school job listings. Students can work in small groups to discuss their various strategies and then report back to the class. Then discuss the questions on page 150 with the class.

The vocabulary task on page 151 presents passages taken from the text. Students should attempt to figure out the meaning of the italicized sections in the passages from the context. If they cannot, they should feel free to use the dictionary. It is important, however, that students practice explaining the meaning of each passage in their own words.

POSTREADING (page 154)

See page vii of this manual for teaching guidelines about postreading.

Think about the Content (page 154)

1 The subject of the article, Agnieszka Ossolinska-Jaskowski, got a job as a paralegal because of her fluency in Polish. The personal-injury firm that hired her was trying to get more clients in New York's Polish-speaking population. (Pars. 1–4)

Bilingual or multilingual nurses are also being recruited by hospitals because it is thought that "a nurse who can talk to a patient in a native language is very important." (Pars. 6–7)

Real estate agencies are also recruiting multilingual workers because they are finding that people who are buying or selling a home find it easier to speak with someone in their primary language. (Pars. 8–10)

Advertising agencies are realizing the benefits of a multilingual workforce. They find that translations of brochures and other materials are more effective when they are done by native speakers of a language. (Par. 11)

2 When Mrs. Jaskowski first began to work for Brand, Brand & Burke, she started off slowly and worked more as an intermediary between Polish-speaking clients and the lawyers in the firm. She did some translations and acted as a translator for clients in situations outside the law office. (Par. 14) After a year, she began making drafts of legal papers and became responsible for deciding "whether a case is good enough for the firm to pursue." (Par. 15) She also "arranges advertising in Polish media and attends events sponsored by her firm in Polish neighborhoods." (Par. 16)

3 Answers may vary.

Think about the Writing (page 154)

1 The author's main idea is that being multilingual or bilingual is an advantage in today's job market. He does not directly state this but instead provides ample evidence to support this point of view.

2 Answers may vary.

3 Both articles give the names of their subjects and begin by telling what they do not have: Berenice Belizaire was not happy. She spoke no English. She lived in a small apartment. Her school life was difficult. Agnieszka Ossolinska-Jaskowski didn't have work experience in the legal field. She didn't have contacts in the legal business. She didn't have a college diploma.

One difference between the two is that Klein only describes Belizaire's problems whereas Skomial also points out Ossolinska-Jaskowski's attribute: She did have fluency in Polish.

Answers to the rest of the question may vary. One thing that students will probably notice is that the main purpose of the introduction in these journalistic essays is to grab the reader's interest. What are we going to find out about Berenice Belizaire? About Agnieszka Ossolinska-Jaskowski? Why are these people worthy subjects for an article? Although the introductions to academic essays often aim to engage the reader's interest, such introductions almost always touch on at least some of the ideas to follow.

4 Skomial implies a question for future study when he writes that seeing Mrs. Jaskowski working as a professional and dressing in a business suit contrasts her with "a typical Polish nanny and a construction worker." The implied question is, "What are the types of jobs usually associated with immigrants and why?" Answers about this may vary.

A Personal Response (page 154)

Answers may vary.

WRITING (pages 155–158)

See page viii of this manual for teaching guidelines about writing.

Journal Writing (page 155)

Remind students to use their journals as a place to reflect and think without worrying about spelling, grammar, or the mechanics of writing.

Formal Writing: *Connecting Ideas* (pages 155–157)

As students become more sophisticated writers, they want to learn strategies for combining sentences, for connecting ideas from one part of an essay to another, and for developing a more fluid, cohesive style of writing. One way to do this is to learn how to connect ideas through transitional words and phrases, keywords, pronouns, and synonyms. As they work through the series of exercises included in this chapter, students will develop skills to make their writing more effective.

FORMAL WRITING PRACTICE 1 (page 156)

Answers may vary. Here are some possible answers. (*S* = Sentence)

Par. 1: *that* (S4 – referring back to "What she did have was fluency in Polish.")

Par. 3: *in fact, recently* (S1 – to show emphasis, to show time)

Par. 4: *A few years ago, so* (S1 – to show time; to explain something); *but* (S2 – to show contrast)

Par. 5: *In the current stumbling economy* (S1 – to show time and to explain something); *And with* (S2 – to explain something)

Par. 7: *but* (S1 – to show contrast); *And even though, when* (S2 – to show contrast, to explain something); *so* (S2 – to show a result)

Par. 9: *because* (S1 – to show a result or connection); *About a month ago, though* (S3 – to show time, to show contrast)

Par. 11: *In the global economy* (S1 – to introduce an additional fact or idea); *Then* (S3 – to show chronological order); *That and other incidents* (S4 – to introduce an additional idea); *In the future* (S5 – to show time)

Par. 13: *At first* (S2 – to show chronological order)

Par. 14: *Early on, but, when* (S1 – to show time and chronological order, to show contrast, to show time); *During the first few months* (S2 – to show chronological order); *even* (S4 – to introduce an additional fact)

Par. 15: *After a year* (S1 – to show time and chronological order); *Although* (S2 – to show contrast); *and that means* (S3 – to show a result)

Par. 16: *When* (S2 – to show a result and time)

Answers will vary. Here are some possible answers.

Words relating to the law
Par. 1: *legal field; legal business; Brand, Brand & Burke, a personal-injury law firm*
Par. 3: *legal issues, the firm*
Par. 4: *the legal profession, a partner at the firm, paralegal*
Par. 12: *the law*
Par. 14: *personal-injury law firm, paralegal certification program, lawyers, full-fledged paralegal, clients, cases*
Par. 15: *clients, legal papers, legal system, a case, the firm*

Words relating to work
See *Formal Writing Practice 4*, page 157.

Words relating to language
Par. 1: *Polish*
Par. 2: *Polish*
Par. 3: *Polish, Polish-language, Polish, Poles, bilingualism*
Par. 4: *Polish, native speaker, English*
Par. 5: *speaking a second language*
Par. 6: *mastery of a foreign tongue, second language, native language*
Par. 7: *Spanish, English, primary language*
Par. 9: *different language groups, English, Spanish, Chinese, Russian, Urdu, Italian*
Par. 10: *Spanish-speaking agents*
Par. 11: *multilingual workforce, Russian, foreign tongue, second language*
Par. 12: *Polish*
Par. 14: *Polish-speaking, Polish, translating, translator*
Par. 15: *Polish*
Par. 16: *Polish*

Words relating to immigration
Par. 2: *been in the United States only for a couple of years, Polish background*
Par. 3: *New York's growing Polish population*
Par. 4: *Polish community, native speaker, immigrant, immigrants*
Par. 5: *immigrants, speaking a second language*
Par. 6: *foreign tongue, native language*
Par. 7: *whose parents emigrated from Puerto Rico, Hispanics*
Par. 8: *multilinguists, ethnic populations*
Par. 9: *many nationalities, emigrated from Hong Kong, newcomers to America, Hispanic couple*
Par. 11: *global economy, ethnic groups in the United States*
Par. 12: *immigrated*
Par. 15: *Polish clients*
Par. 16: *Polish neighborhoods*

1 *Agnieszka Ossolinska-Jaskowski* didn't have work experience in the legal
   field. She didn't have any important contacts in the legal business. And she
   didn't yet have a diploma from Montclair State University in New Jersey,
   where she was studying to be a paralegal. What she did have was fluency
   in Polish. And that was enough to get her a job at Brand, Brand & Burke, a
   personal-injury law firm in Manhattan.
   (All the pronouns refer to the antecedent *Agnieszka Ossolinska-Jaskowski.*)

2 *The hiring managers* at the Presbyterian Hospital in New York, which
   employs people from 88 countries, say *they* consider mastery of a foreign
   tongue a strong plus.
   (The pronoun *they* refers to the antecedent *The hiring managers.*)

3 *Ms. Sánchez-Vega*, a registered nurse who was born in the United States
   but whose parents emigrated from Puerto Rico, is the only nurse of 18 who
   can speak Spanish. And even though *most Hispanics* who are admitted
   speak English, *they* feel more at ease when *she* speaks to them in *Spanish*,
   she says. "*It* is *their* primary language, so *they* naturally prefer to use *it*
   rather than English."
   (The pronoun *she* refers to the antecedent *Ms. Sánchez-Vega*. The pronouns
   they, their, and *they* refer to the antecedent *most Hispanics*. The pronoun *it*
   refers to the antecedent *Spanish.*)

4 *Mr. Ma*, who *himself* emigrated from Hong Kong, said many of *his*
   customers were newcomers to America who spoke little or no English.
   About a month ago, *a Hispanic couple* came to *his* office, and though
   they couldn't understand English, kept repeating the phrase, "*We* want sell
   home."
   (The pronouns *himself, his,* and *his* refer to the antecedent *Mr. Ma*. The
   pronouns *they* and *We* refer to the antecedent *a Hispanic couple.*)

5 *Mark Levit*, a managing partner at Partners & Levit, a Manhattan advertising
   agency, says that while the firm has overseas clients and creates ads aimed
   at specific ethnic groups in the United States, *his* only requirement for hiring
   a bookkeeper used to be accounting skills. Then, one day, *his bookkeeper,
   a Russian woman*, told him that in *her* view a Russian translation that *she*
   had seen of a Partners & Levit brochure was better than the original.
   (The pronouns *his, his,* and *him* refer to the antecedent *Mark Levit*. The
   pronouns *her* and *she* refer to the antecedent *his bookkeeper, a Russian
   woman.*)

6 *Mrs. Jaskowski* arranges advertising in Polish media and attends events sponsored by her firm in Polish neighborhoods. When *the residents* see *her* in a business suit, *she* says, "It makes *them* rethink the image of a typical Polish nanny and a construction worker."
(The pronouns *her, her,* and *she* refer to the antecedent *Mrs. Jaskowski*. The pronoun *them* refers to the antecedent *the residents*.)

FORMAL WRITING PRACTICE 4 (page 157)

Answers may vary. Here are some possible answers.

Par. 1: *work experience, legal field, paralegal, job, personal-injury law firm*
Par. 3: *position, job*
Par. 4: *profession, employees, partner, worked, hiring, paralegal, on-the-job training*
Par. 5: *economy, job seekers, qualification, employers, field*
Par. 6: *nursing, hiring managers, employs, senior vice president, chief of human resources, nurse*
Par. 7: *job, registered nurse, nurse*
Par. 8: *real estate, field, payroll, firms*
Par. 9: *hiring, customers, firm, president, owner, office*
Par. 10: *Spanish-speaking agents, office*
Par. 11: *economy, companies, workforce, managing partner, advertising agency, firm, clients, hiring, bookkeeper, skills, employee, hiring criterion*
Par. 12: *teacher, weekend school, job, employer*
Par. 13: *job*
Par. 14: *pay, experience, personal-injury firm, job, lawyers, paralegal, tasks, clients, doctor, translator*
Par. 15: *job, clients, tasks, firm, work*
Par. 16: *work, business suit, nanny, construction worker*

Formal Writing: *Writing a Response Essay* (pages 157–158)

In many college classes, students are required to write response essays. In this chapter, they work on what this kind of assignment entails and how they should go about it. The writing assignment asks students to respond to the reading in this chapter or to other readings in this book. If you prefer – or for additional practice – you can assign a response paper to an essay from a newspaper or magazine, a short story, or a longer piece of writing. You may want students to write their response essays on a class Web board where they can read each other's work. In any case, be sure to have at least several students respond to the same reading. This will give them the opportunity to see the many possible ways to respond to the same content.

Getting Started: *Brainstorming in a Small Group* (page 158)

In Chapter 6, students got started by brainstorming on their own. Here they will be doing it with a small group. The advantage of working with a group is the variety of ideas and associations each student will discover.

REVISING (pages 159–160)

See page ix of this manual for teaching guidelines about revising.

Make sure students discuss in what ways "Job Satisfaction and Today's World" either satisfies or does not satisfy the format described on page 158 of the Student's Book.

EDITING (pages 161–165)

See page x of this manual for teaching guidelines about editing.

Grammar: *Modals* (pages 161–165)

Learning to use modals effectively is extremely important because we use them so much in both speaking and writing. What makes modals difficult at first is the rule that the verb following the modal has no inflectional ending whether it is being used in the first, second, or third person. Once students understand this, modals become easier to use correctly.

GRAMMAR PRACTICE 1 (page 164)

Answers may vary.
You might want to photocopy the groups' paragraphs, distribute them, and discuss them as a class.

GRAMMAR PRACTICE 2 (page 164)

Answers may vary.

GRAMMAR PRACTICE 3 (page 164)

See *Answer Key* in Student's Book, page 242.

Mechanics: *The Semicolon and the Colon* (pages 165–166)

Students sometimes confuse semicolons and commas, so it may be useful to suggest that students review Chapter 5 (pages 95–97) for comma rules.

MECHANICS PRACTICE (page 166)

See *Answer Key* in Student's Book, page 242.

UNIT FOUR
Roots

....
BACK, BUT NOT HOME

"Back, but Not Home" is written by Maria L. Muñiz, who was born in Cuba and has not returned there since she immigrated to the United States when she was nearly five years old. Muñiz's situation is complicated by the fact that the home she left is politically problematic for the United States.

PREREADING (pages 168–169)

See page vi of this manual for teaching guidelines about prereading and reading.

Begin by discussing the illustration on page 168. How important are photos of family and friends to your students? What types of photos do they keep? Has the world of digital photography affected the kinds of photos they take, give to others, and keep for posterity? How many of them have video cameras and use these to record family events? Some teachers extend discussion of the illustration by asking students to bring a photo of themselves (perhaps a baby picture), family, or friends to class. You can have students write about the significance of the photo for them and then share both the photo and the writing with a small group. If you do this, consider having students display their photos around the room before they share their writing and let the class guess to which student each photo belongs.

Discuss the questions on page 168. Here is some information that may be useful for the second question.

Cuba is a Caribbean island about 90 miles south of the Florida Keys. After 1492, when Christopher Columbus landed in Cuba, it became a Spanish colony. The Spanish developed coffee and sugar plantations and imported Africans to work on them. Thus, Cuba's population, which today numbers about 12,000,000, consists mainly of descendents of the Spanish colonists, African slaves, and indigenous peoples.

After the Spanish-American War of 1898, Cuba became independent, but the United States was a dominant influence. From the 1920s until 1959, Cuba existed under various dictators, notably Fulgencio

Batista, who ruled Cuba from 1940 to 1959. Fidel Castro overthrew Batista in 1959, and he remains in power today. Castro established a socialist government with strong ties to the communist Soviet Union. In 1961, because of Castro's relationship with the former Soviet Union, the United States placed an embargo on trade with Cuba that is still in effect. Then, in 1990, the Soviet Union withdrew many of its former subsidies. As a result of the Soviet's withdrawal of aid and the U.S. embargo, Cuba has suffered severe economic problems that continue until this day.

Over the years since Castro took power, many Cubans have attempted to escape to the United States. The most famous attempt occurred in 1980 when about 125,000 refugees in small boats tried to sail across the Straits of Florida to the United States from Mariel, Cuba, in what became known as the Cuban Boat Lift.

The vocabulary task on page 169 presents passages taken from the text. Students should attempt to figure out the meaning of the italicized words in the passages from the context. If they cannot, they should feel free to use the dictionary. It is important, however, that students practice explaining the meaning of each passage in their own words.

POSTREADING (pages 171–172)

See page vii of this manual for teaching guidelines about postreading.

Think about the Content (page 171)

Answers may vary. Here are some possible answers for 1–3.

1 The author has lived in New York since she was nearly five years old. She finds the world in Miami to be quite different from the one she knows in New York; Miami is more like Cuba. In Miami she has been accused of being too Americanized, so she has been made to feel like an outsider. It is troubling to be of Cuban background but not to feel accepted by the Cuban population in Miami. This is an illustration of how Muñiz is an outsider and insider at the same time – a person with a dual identity searching for her true self.

2 Muñiz had difficulty speaking English when she entered the United States, and she was not treated well in school. Although she understood much of what was said around her, she did not express herself well and was made fun of by schoolmates. She was put in the slowest reading classes. Her teachers' surprise when she did do well hurt almost as much as their expectation that she would do poorly. She felt she always had to prove she "was as good as the others," and as she grew up, "it became a matter of pride to prove [she] was better than the others."

3 Muñiz wants to return to Cuba because she is a person with a divided sense of self. She identifies as Cuban or Cuban American, but she has not been to Cuba since she was a very young child. She has not seen much of her family since that time, but she dreams about them and misses what she had to give up. Yet she is a successful American woman – a woman torn between two worlds.

Think about the Writing (page 171)

Answers may vary. Here are some possible answers for 1–3.

1 Her one-word answer, "Yes," is powerful because it is unequivocal even though her experiences are more problematic. This strong answer tells the reader that the writer is a person who has thought through her problem and reached her answer, although it was not without much pain and confusion. Writers rarely write one-word sentences, and they should not be used frivolously. They must be about something important that needs to stand out and make a strong point.

2 The third paragraph consists of the words *Outside American, inside Cuban.* This is a powerful sentence and deserves to stand alone, although writers very rarely write one-sentence paragraphs. In fact, the idea that this is so unusual in writing adds literary strength to it. It expresses the torn feelings of the writer and her allegiances to two countries and ways of life.

3 The "missing piece" is Cuba itself – the land, the people, her family. She needs to find that piece of herself that she left behind as a small frightened child, and it makes sense that she find it now as a strong, successful young adult. Students will probably find the conclusion effective.

A Personal Response (page 172)

Answers may vary.

WRITING (pages 172–174)

See page viii of this manual for teaching guidelines about writing.

Journal Writing (page 172)

Remind students to use their journals as a place to reflect and think without worrying about spelling, grammar, or the mechanics of writing.

Formal Writing: *Cause-and-Effect Essay* (pages 172–174)

Students are provided with guidelines for two approaches to using cause and effect: one beginning with the cause and the other beginning with the effect. (See page 173.) They will find it useful to practice both and will probably find that one technique works better with particular subjects than the other.

In Chapter 9, students worked on using transitional words and phrases (pages 155–156). Writing a cause-and-effect essay is another good opportunity to practice this skill.

Getting Started: *Structured Freewriting* (page 174)

Students were introduced to freewriting in Chapter 1, but here they will modify freewriting to include a topic. Many students enjoy this technique and find that it really helps them with their essay writing.

REVISING (pages 174–176)

See page ix of this manual for teaching guidelines about revising.

One aspect of "Outside/Inside" that students may question is the very personal voice that the writer brings to her subject. Ask students whether they think it is appropriate, and for which audience(s) it may be appropriate. Students need to think about audience every time they write, and this essay may give them a forum to discuss some of the issues that emerge.

EDITING (pages 176–179)

See page x of this manual for teaching guidelines about editing.

Grammar: *Adverbial Clauses* (pages 176–179)

As students are encouraged to combine sentences and to create more complex embedded sentences, they need to learn the use of adverbial clauses – clauses that use subordinating conjunctions such as *when*, *because*, and *although*. These are so important to making connections in writing, yet in trying to use these clauses, students sometimes create either fragments or run-on sentences. If you find your students doing this, you can review with them the *Mechanics* section in Chapter 7 ("Run-on Sentences and Comma Splices") and the *Mechanics* section in Chapter 8 ("Fragments").

GRAMMAR PRACTICE 1 (page 177)

Answers may vary. Here are some possible answers.

1 *since*	4 *because*
2 *As; because*	5 *although*
3 *Even though; as soon as*	6 *Because*

GRAMMAR PRACTICE 2 (page 178)

Answers may vary.

Here is a partial list of sentences containing adverbial clauses in the Muñiz article. The adverbial clauses are contained in brackets and the words in italics are subordinating conjunctions that signal the beginning of the clause. Since there are many adverbial clauses in the article, you might want to put students in small groups and ask each group to look for the sentences in different paragraphs.

Notice that in the examples from paragraphs 5, 6, and 8 below Muñiz has not always included commas according to the rules. The missing commas are circled. You can remind students that although professional writers may break the rules from time to time, students must follow the rules to demonstrate that they know them.

Paragraph 2
I came to the United States with my parents [*when* I was almost five years old.]
I often feel awkward visiting relatives in Miami [*because* it is such a different world.]
Yet, [*although* I am now an American citizen,] [*whenever* anyone has asked me my nationality,] I have always and unhesitatingly replied "Cuban."

Paragraph 4
We talked of Cuban politics and [*although* the discussion was very casual,] I felt an old anger welling inside.
[*After* 16 years of living an "American" life,] I am still unable to view the revolution with detachment or objectivity.

Paragraph 5
And [*as* I listened to this man talk of the Cuban situation,] I began to remember how as a little girl I would wake up crying [*because* I had dreamed of my aunts and grandmothers⊙ and I missed them.]
I remembered my mother's trembling voice and the sad look on her face [*whenever* she spoke to her mother over the phone.]
And [*as* the conversation continued,] I began to remember how difficult it often was to grow up Latina in an American world.

Paragraph 6
I'd been in this country only a few months⊙ and [*although* I understood a good deal of what was said to me,] I could not express myself very well.
I felt so helpless [*because* inside I was crying.]

Paragraph 7
[*As* I grew a little older,] Latina meant being automatically relegated to the slowest reading classes in school.
[*By now* my English was fluent,] but the teachers would always assume I was somewhat illiterate or slow.
[*As* a child,] I began to realize that Latina would always mean proving I was as good as the others.

[*As* I grew older,] it became a matter of pride to prove I was better than the others.

Paragraph 8
[*As* an adult] I have come to terms with these memories and they don't hurt as much.

Paragraph 9
And this is why [*when* I am now asked, "Do you want to go back?"] I say "yes" with conviction.

Paragraph 10
I have to return to Cuba one day [*because* I want to know that little girl better.]

Paragraph 11
[*When* I try to review my life during the past 16 years,] I almost feel as if I've walked into a theater right in the middle of a movie.
And I'm afraid I won't fully understand or enjoy the rest of the movie [*unless* I can see and understand the beginning.]

Paragraph 13
I want to return [*because* the journey back will also mean a journey within.]

GRAMMAR PRACTICE 4 (page 178)

See *Answer Key* in Student's Book, page 243.

Mechanics: *Parallelism* (pages 179–180)

The concept that words or phrases presented in series should be parallel in structure is a difficult one for many students. Once you have reviewed the discussion and the practice on pages 179–180, you may want students to look at some of their own essays or other essays in the book to examine parallelism and how it works in actual writing.

MECHANICS PRACTICE (page 180)

See *Answer Key* in Student's Book, page 243.

Chapter Eleven

LEGACIES

"Legacies," by Alejandro Portes and Rubén G. Rumbaut, is an excerpt from their book *Legacies: The Story of the Immigrant Second Generation*, which exposes students to new vocabulary and ideas dealing with demographics and immigration.

Allow plenty of time to work on this chapter because students will find it challenging. The reading is an academic text with densely packed information and statistics, the *Writing Assignment* is a research paper, and the *Mechanics* section introduces students to documenting their research.

PREREADING (pages 181–182)

See page vi of this manual for teaching guidelines about prereading and reading.

In this chapter, you might begin by discussing the questions on page 181 before addressing the illustration. Question 3 asks if the most recent wave of immigrants is successful. You may want to add to that a question about what success means in this context. Then ask your students to look at the illustration on page 181. What does the person see in the mirror? What do they think this illustration suggests about legacies? It is very likely that the discussion will lead to the issue of how we identify ourselves. If the discussion does go in that direction – or if you lead it that way – ask students to individually list the first five terms that occur to them in relation to the way they identify themselves. Often people list such terms as male/female, married/unmarried, ethnic background, or racial background. Collate the categories students mention on the board. Each time that the same category is mentioned, put a check next to it. Then discuss the results of this survey. How do most students in the class identify themselves and why? What is the least common means of identification? Does our identity change based on our audience (as we have said our writing style does)? Does our identity vary when we are in different situations? This can lead to an interesting discussion and a possible writing assignment: What is identity, and how do we define ourselves?

The vocabulary task on page 182 presents passages taken from the text. Students should attempt to figure out the meaning of the italicized sections in the passages from the context. If they cannot, they should feel free to use the dictionary. It is important, however, that students practice explaining the meaning of each passage in their own words.

POSTREADING (pages 188–189)

See page vii of this manual for teaching guidelines about postreading.

Think about the Content (page 188)

1 "Because the size of [the population of immigrant children] is driven by the influx of immigrants, it has grown rapidly in the 1990s and will expand further at the beginning of the twenty-first century." (Par. 4)

"Immigrant children and U.S.-born children of immigrants are the fastest-growing segment of the country's total population of children under 18 years of age." (Par. 5)

Table 2.1, on page 185, illustrates this fact.

"The rapid rise and concentration of this population reflects the accelerated rate of recent immigration to the United States." (Par. 6)

"The youthfulness of today's immigrant population is another salient feature." (Par. 7)

Paragraph 8 continues to give statistics "confirm[ing] the relative youth of this population."

2 Immigrants tend to settle in large urban areas where previous immigrants from their countries have established communities. Answers may vary as to the significance of this fact. Depending on how one views it, the significance may be that schools and other public institutions will learn from the new immigrant population about different cultures and ways of life. On the other hand, some may view this concentration of immigrants as creating a problem for areas with limited resources.

3 The significance is that we will not know how successful this generation will be until we see how they "cop[e] with the challenges of growing up in an environment foreign to themselves or to their parents." (Par. 9)

4 Answers may vary. One possible answer is that if these young people are viewed positively and given the resources necessary to meet their family, health, and educational needs, they will be a tremendous asset to the country. If they do not receive these resources, they may not become productive and positive members of society.

Think about the Writing (page 188)

Answers may vary.

A Personal Response (pages 188–189)

Answers may vary.

WRITING (pages 189–193)

See page viii of this manual for teaching guidelines about writing.

Journal Writing (page 189)

Remind students to use their journals as a place to reflect and think without worrying about spelling, grammar, or the mechanics of writing.

Formal Writing: *Introduction to Writing a Research Paper* (pages 189–190)

Increasingly, students are asked to write short research papers in the first year of college. In this chapter, they are given the opportunity to develop the skills required for researching, writing, and citing a short paper.

Getting Started: *Finding Sources* (pages 190–193)

In this section, students are introduced to the various resources available for doing research: the library with books, periodicals, and databases; the Internet with its databases and search engines. It is important that students gain experience using both libraries and the Internet to prepare them for future college courses.

In this section, students are shown which information to note for each source that they research. Then in the *Mechanics* section, they are shown how to formulate their documentation. Make sure students understand that they should take down the information for every source they look at even though they are not sure whether they will use it. It is much easier to take down the documentation information for a source you may not use than to go back and try to find it again later if you change your mind.

REVISING (pages 193–196)

See page ix of this manual for teaching guidelines about revising.

When students read the sample research paper on pages 194–196, do not go into detail or let your students ask too many questions about the method of documentation. Remind students that they will learn the guidelines for correct documentation in the *Mechanics* section.

EDITING (pages 196–209)

See page x of this manual for teaching guidelines about editing.

Grammar: *Verbals* (pages 196–202)

The correct use of gerunds, infinitives, participles, and participial phrases is a skill that students need to expand the scope of their writing.

GRAMMAR PRACTICE 1 (pages 197–198)

Answers may vary. Here are some possible answers.

1 *talking*
2 *Eating*
3 *Working together / Participating*
4 *learning*
5 *Studying*

GRAMMAR PRACTICE 2 (page 199)

Answers may vary. Here are some possible answers.

1 *to study; to get*
2 *to buy; to find*
3 *to have*
4 *To sing (well)*
5 *to take*
6 *to drive*

Answers may vary. Here are some possible answers.

1 *to work*	4 *meeting*
2 *to bring*	5 *to pay*
3 *using*	

GRAMMAR PRACTICE 4 (page 201)

Answers may vary.

GRAMMAR PRACTICE 5 (page 201)

Answers may vary.

GRAMMAR PRACTICE 6 (pages 201–202)

See *Answer Key* in Student's Book, page 243.

Mechanics: *The MLA System* (pages 202–205)
The APA System (pages 206–209)

Students may find this information overwhelming at first. Point out that they do not have to memorize it; they should become familiar with the general idea, and understand that they can return to these pages or consult a writer's handbook or online help site as necessary.

MECHANICS PRACTICE 1 (page 209)

See *Answer Key* in Student's Book, on page 244.

MECHANICS PRACTICE 2 (page 209)

Be prepared to tell your students which documentation system you want them to use.

Chapter Twelve

THE MAN TO SEND RAIN CLOUDS

"The Man to Send Rain Clouds," by Leslie Marmon Silko, is a short story that examines cultural conflicts between traditional Native Americans and Christians after the death of a Native American elder.

PREREADING (pages 211–212)

See page vi of this manual for teaching guidelines about prereading and reading.

Begin by asking students to write for a few minutes about the person in the illustration on page 211. Who is he, where is he, and what is he thinking? Suggest to students that they try to associate the illustration with the title of the story. Ask some students to read what they have written aloud (either to the class or in small groups). Then discuss the questions on page 211 with the class.

The vocabulary task on page 212, *Vocabulary: Specialized Words*, is different in this chapter because the short story includes special words that relate either to the southwestern United States or to the Roman Catholic religion, and it is not expected that most students would be able to guess the meanings of these words from context. After students have looked up the words, discussed them, and read the story once, you may want to return to the lists of specialized words and see if students remember the meanings and the contexts in which each was used. For example, an *arroyo* is the path along which water flows in an arid region; in dry seasons, the arroyo may have no water. Elicit from students the information that the word *arroyo* is used in paragraph 1 of the story because the old man was found dead in a "wide, sandy arroyo." Following this procedure with the remaining words can help students remember details of the story.

POSTREADING (pages 216–217)

See page vii of this manual for teaching guidelines about postreading.

Think about the Content (page 216)

1 Paragraphs 2 and 11 describe how Teofilo's body was prepared for burial. After the preparation, he was wrapped in a blanket and buried in a community-dug grave with no coffin. (Par. 36) In paragraph 31, the priest explains the minimum requirements for a Roman Catholic burial: "There should have been the Last Rites and a funeral Mass at the very least."

2–5 Answers may vary.

Think about the Writing (page 217)

Answers may vary. In question 1, however, students should notice that each section represents a different time of day. Ask them to find the sentence in each section that tells (approximately) what time it is.

A Personal Response (page 217)

Answers may vary.

WRITING (pages 217–219)

See page viii of this manual for teaching guidelines about writing.

Journal Writing (page 217)

Remind students to use their journals as a place to reflect and think without worrying about spelling, grammar, or the mechanics of writing.

Formal Writing: *Introduction to Writing about Literature* (pages 218–219)

In many literature classes, students are asked to write about what they have read. This chapter offers students an introduction to typical ways of analyzing and responding to literature, specifically: exploring a theme, describing the plot, analyzing characters, interpreting symbols, and examining the social context in which the piece takes place. It is important to make clear to students that these approaches often overlap. In other words, though a student may be primarily interested in discussing a particular character, inevitably he or she will need to refer to the theme, the plot, a symbol, the social context, or all of these.

Students need to support their views using the same tools they do when writing an essay, academic study, or research paper: summarizing, paraphrasing, quoting, and giving examples. And if they choose to read scholarly interpretations of the work and incorporate these views into their essays, they will need to cite them correctly.

Formal Writing Practice on page 219 asks students to practice responding to literature with "The All-American Slurp," which they read in Chapter 6. If you think your students would benefit from practicing with "The Man to Send Rain Clouds" before they write their essays about it, you can either substitute "Rain Clouds" for "Slurp" or have them practice with both stories.

Getting Started: *Clustering* (page 220)

In order to get the most out of clustering, students usually need some practice. Give them time to analyze the cluster on page 220 that is based on "The All-American Slurp." Draw their attention to the fact that the creator of the cluster isn't sure whether the topic he or she wants to address – food – is the theme of the story or a symbol in the story. Discuss with students which they think it is and why. You might want to put on the board another cluster developed by your students based on a different aspect of "The All-American Slurp," for example, a cluster based on the character of the narrator.

After students have completed the first four steps of the activity, you might photocopy some of their clusters, distribute them, and discuss them as a class before they proceed to step 5, that is, before they begin to plan their essays.

REVISING (pages 221–222)

See page ix of this manual for teaching guidelines about revising.

The literary response paper, "The Man to Send Rain Clouds," was chosen because of the writer's understanding of the short story and his ability to combine a quotation, a deep analysis of the story, and his personal experience into one well-developed essay. Students may find his language challenging, but they should see in it an effective response to a short story.

EDITING (pages 223–225)

See page x of this manual for teaching guidelines about editing.

Grammar: *Indirect Speech* (pages 223–225)

This section introduces guidelines for writing indirect speech, something we do all the time when we talk and tell each other stories about what others have said. Read through the guidelines on page 223 with your students. After they have completed the grammar practices, you can give them additional practice by having two or three students "perform" a conversation about something and letting the class put it into indirect speech. Ask students to tell you which type of speech (direct or indirect) is mainly used in "The All-American Slurp" and "The Man to Send Rain Clouds." Then discuss why they think direct speech (the correct answer) is used. You might ask them which of the nonfiction pieces in the book make use of direct speech, and why.

Be prepared for students to tell you that they hear "like" instead of "said" in indirect speech (e.g., "He was like, 'Are you coming to the party?'"). This is a commonly used expression in speaking, but it is not acceptable in formal written English unless you are quoting someone or writing dialogue for a character who speaks this way.

GRAMMAR PRACTICE 1 (page 224)

1 Maria said that she had left Cuba when she was five years old.
2 The college president said that some students worried about high tuitions.
3 Alevtina said that she could speak Russian and Uzbek.
4 The teacher said that Ming would present her paper the next day.
5 The couple announced that they had just gotten their marriage license.
6 Juan asked when the final would be.

GRAMMAR PRACTICE 2 (page 224)

Answers may vary.

GRAMMAR PRACTICE 3 (pages 224–225)

See *Answer Key* in Student's Book, page 245.

Mechanics: *Word Order in Describing Nouns* (pages 225–227)

The chart on page 225 illustrates the general order for words that describe nouns. Students usually find this interesting and enjoy doing the practice exercises. When they do their own writing, some of them may become self-conscious and look up the "proper" order in the chart. Over time they will become more comfortable using series of descriptive words and even more familiar with hearing the correct order; however, the chart is something they can always fall back on as a guide.

MECHANICS PRACTICE 1 (pages 225–226)

1 They found him under a big cottonwood tree. (Par. 1)

2 Leon took a piece of string out of his pocket and tied a small gray feather in the old man's long white hair. (Par. 2)

3 The red plaid shawl had been shaken and spread carefully over the bed, and a new brown flannel shirt and a pair of stiff new Levis were arranged neatly beside the pillow. (Par. 11)

4 Louise stood outside with her hands in the pockets of Leon's green army jacket that was too big for her. (Par. 15)

5 The wind pulled at the priest's brown Franciscan robe and swirled away the cornmeal and pollen that had been sprinkled on the blanket. (Par. 36)

6 Leon watched him climb the hill, and when he had disappeared within the tall, thick walls, Leon turned to look up at the high blue mountains in the deep snow that reflected a faint red light from the west. (Par. 36)

MECHANICS PRACTICE 2 (page 226)

Answers may vary.

MECHANICS PRACTICE 3 (page 226)

See *Answer Key* in Student's Book, page 245.

CPSIA information can be obtained at www.ICGtesting.com
Printed in the USA
LVOW10s1922010414

379876LV00002B/41/P